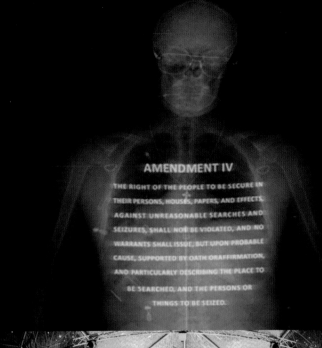

(This music is embedded from YouTube. View Original The Artist is not a participant in or sponsor of this website.)

Newsjacking

The Urgent Genius of Real-Time Advertising

Grant Hunter and

Jon Burkhart

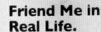

Friend Me in Real Life.

Wanna hang out? I don't have a computer or Facebook, but you can look me in the eye, if you're up for it.

🔁 **Thames & Hudson**

Contents

On the cover, front: Newsjacking Gun concept by Grant Hunter, created by Creased Lightning, retouched by Joe Kerrigan. Back, top: 'Kit Kat Longest Match' by JWT London (see page 25); bottom: 'Polo Snow Stamp' by JWT London (see page 33).

First published in the United Kingdom in 2013 by Thames & Hudson Ltd, 181A High Holborn, London WC1V 7QX

Newsjacking © 2013 Grant Hunter and Jon Burkhart

Designed by Andy Nethercleft and Grant Hunter

British Library Cataloguing-in-Publication Data A catalogue record for this book is available from the British Library

ISBN 978-0-500-51672-0

Printed and bound in China by Everbest Printing Co. Ltd.

To find out about all our publications, please visit **www.thamesandhudson.com**. There you can subscribe to our e-newsletter, browse or download our current catalogue, and buy any titles that are in print.

SLAP NICK GRIFFIN

Introduction

In many ways the book you hold in your hands is a huge contradiction. We like it that way. Who would expect real-time digital creativity to be housed in an old-fashioned printed tome with huge lead times? It's the antithesis of our own little contradiction-in-terms Urgent Genius. One more contradiction: this newsjacking movement has been equally inspired by Steve Jobs and Paris Hilton. One moment, we feel like

'Why join the navy if you can be a pirate?' Steve Jobs

'think-different' pirates jumping off a sinking advertising ship. The next moment, we take our brazen, misguided confidence into places we shouldn't be allowed to go.

And tomorrow, we'll be inspired by two totally different people. That's how fast technology has increased the pace of modern life. But in doing so it's liberated creativity, allowing individuals to release their genius at an equally frenetic speed.

For the last couple of years our blog, urgentgenius.com, has celebrated these timely creations from around the globe. It has evolved from a simple collection of the best real-

'It will work. I am a marketing genius.' Paris Hilton

time work into a global network of creatives who embrace the Urgent Genius mindset in everything they do. A printed book – tactile and analogue but digitally connected through QR codes – seemed the best way to celebrate the geniuses we've discovered along the way.

Our journey started in October 2009 with inspiration from an unlikely source – a far-right politician. Nick Griffin is the leader of the British National Party, a political organization in the UK. His appearance on the highly regarded BBC show *Question Time* spread discontent in the UK about the decision to allow him on prime-time national television. Griffin's appearance turned into a public mauling of the man and his policies, but large sections of the public were still concerned that the BBC had given Griffin a platform for his extreme views in the first place.

Jon Plackett, a London-based advertising creative, was so incensed by Griffin's rhetoric that as soon as the show had finished he was compelled to act. He found a piece of video of Griffin addressing a Ku Klux Klan rally in Texas, then designed, wrote and coded a site

built around it called slapnickgriffin.com. It simply allowed users to slap Griffin in the face while recording the total number of slaps.

Around 7 a.m. the following day, he uploaded the site to a B3ta.com message board. It soon went viral and even earned him death threats from extremists. Less than a week later, Jon was celebrating a site that enjoyed a few broken servers and 25 million slaps – the first time we witnessed the power of Urgent Genius. During the research for this book we've uncovered other amazing ideas, so we will set the scene with a few favourites from the last decade.

SPEARS 55 HOUR SHOCKER

Lynx Britney Wedding – 2004

Our first example comes from 3 January 2004. On a night out in Las Vegas, Britney Spears married childhood sweetheart Jason Alexander. Dressed in jeans and baseball caps, it was apparently 'spur of the moment...a wild thing'. The singer's lawyers moved instantly to get the marriage quashed, claiming that: 'Britney lacked understanding of her actions and was incapable of agreeing to the marriage.' Within fifty-five hours, the marriage was null and void. BBH London conceived, designed, planned and published this ad all within twenty-four hours to ensure it ran in the newspapers just a day after the story broke.

We respectfully ask Prime Minister John Howard to sit on it.

JERRIK swivel chair with armrests $569

Prime Minister John Howard wants to spend almost $3000 on a single chair while this one here offers quality, design and comfort for only $569. In fact, our range of chairs starts from as low as $12.95. Surely that would make us the preferred choice.

©Inter IKEA Systems B.V. 2007. While stocks last

IKEA®

Spend less. Live more.

IKEA John Howard Chairs – 2007

On 22 May 2007, the *Sydney Morning Herald* revealed the government had planned to spend in excess of $200,000 on executive chairs for the cabinet offices of the Prime Minister. Liberal backbencher Don Randall defended the expenditure:

'Do you really want him to go off to IKEA and get his Allen key out and put together a heap of dodgy chairs for people to sit on?'

Host Sydney spotted the opportunity for IKEA to respond and created a quarter-page tactical ad in the *Sydney Morning Herald*. The $10,000 media investment resulted in around $500,000 worth of PR – the ad featured on every Australian news channel and it also made the letters page of the *Sydney Morning Herald*.

Veet Goodbye Bush – 2009

In January 2009, the 'Goodbye Bush' ad created by EURO RSCG appeared in the *Sydney Daily Telegraph* and *Melbourne Herald Sun*. Veet, for those who don't know, is a hair-removal product. Due to its global popularity, after Australians scanned the ad in and forwarded it to friends online, the ad was placed in publications in New Zealand and Canada. It went on to win an Australian Caxton newspaper award. According to Steve Coll, the current Executive Creative Director, it took tenacity from the then-ECD, Rowan Dean, to sell the idea to Veet: he presented the ad to his client in a cafe and asked the other female customers to confirm it wasn't offensive. This was enough to finally persuade the client to run it.

20% OFF
ALL GARAGE DOORS*

*TOYOTA OWNERS ONLY

DPT
DANSKPORTTEKNIK.DK

DPT Garage Doors – 2010

2010 was not a good year for Toyota: they announced the global recall of over 10 million vehicles. Problems ranged from faulty brakes to dodgy fuel pumps and sticking accelerator pedals. JWT Copenhagen created this cheeky ad for DPT garage doors. Poking fun at Toyota's sticking accelerator pedals, the ad took just one week to go from conception to publication. Both the agency and client were nervous about any potential fatalities coming from the faulty pedals. If that had happened the potential backlash for DPT could have been huge. It took courage to commit to the ad and it paid off. The ad picked up widespread coverage across press titles in Denmark and around the globe.

'Consumers want directions now, search now, movie reviews now personalized news now, sports scores now.... Consumers are creating or clamouring for content that is personalized, shareable and available anytime, anyplace, anywhere.'

Macy & Thompson

As you can see, we really do appreciate topical ads. As two creatives, we love the rush of having an idea with an expiration date. It forces people to make a decision. It means that we get to go out and make something that won't get killed by a regional focus group, because there's simply no time for that process to take place. The client must either trust the idea, or stop it dead in its tracks.

That said, time scales have changed. Overnight's not good enough any more, because in the morning it's too late. The net has turbocharged our media consumption, and agencies must adjust accordingly.

Luckily our tools are better, too. You can now stay up all night to write, code, record, edit and send your brilliance out to the world in a matter of hours.

The BBC did some research that proved that we all have nine-second attention spans. Blame social media: we all want it now and we won't wait. As Beverly Macy and Teri Thompson state in their book *The Power of Real-time Social Media Marketing*, consumers want it all now.

So if it doesn't bowl us over, we've moved on to the next tweet. Why are we like this? Well, we've been overloaded. Hit from all sides. Our brains are exploding, and it's the only way to cope.

How overloaded are our brains? This quote from Google CEO Eric Schmidt in 2010 says it all:

'We now generate as much information every two days as was generated from the beginning of time to 2003.' E. Schmidt

Schmidt made that statement back in 2010; the sheer volume of content we're now generating is staggering. The signal-to-noise ratio (useful information versus background chatter) is changing radically. At the start of 2012, YouTube released statistics stating that every second, one hour of video gets uploaded to the video portal.

'Every second one hour of video gets uploaded to YouTube…. That's a decade of video every single day.' YouTube

If you want to get noticed among all this clutter, you have to generate ideas that truly stand out. If they are 'of the moment', they're more likely to be successful. They need to capture the zeitgeist. Content was king, now content within context rules the waves.

It's what we call Urgent Genius.

Urgent Genius –
The principles

We started tracking the Urgent Genius trend at the end of 2009. During that time we've discovered brilliant work from around the world. As we collected and created work, it became clear that there are underlying principles to an Urgent Genius mindset. It's a philosophy anyone can adopt but many struggle to implement. With that in mind, we've grouped the work under seven guiding themes, each with a chapter dedicated to showing real-world examples that bring the theory to life. It's worth noting that many of the case studies display more than one of our tenets, but for simplicity's sake we've grouped them under the one that demonstrates it best.

Each chapter starts with a detailed description of the work followed by interviews with some of the creators, as well as illustrations to help show the key points. The case studies then follow in full colour to show the core components of each idea. The QR code at the start of each chapter will take you to further digital content, giving additional background should you want to know more. The book documents the journey we've been on so far and it's a journey that continues to pick up pace. We hope you enjoy using this book as a reference tool as much as we have enjoyed researching and creating it.

Grant & Jon

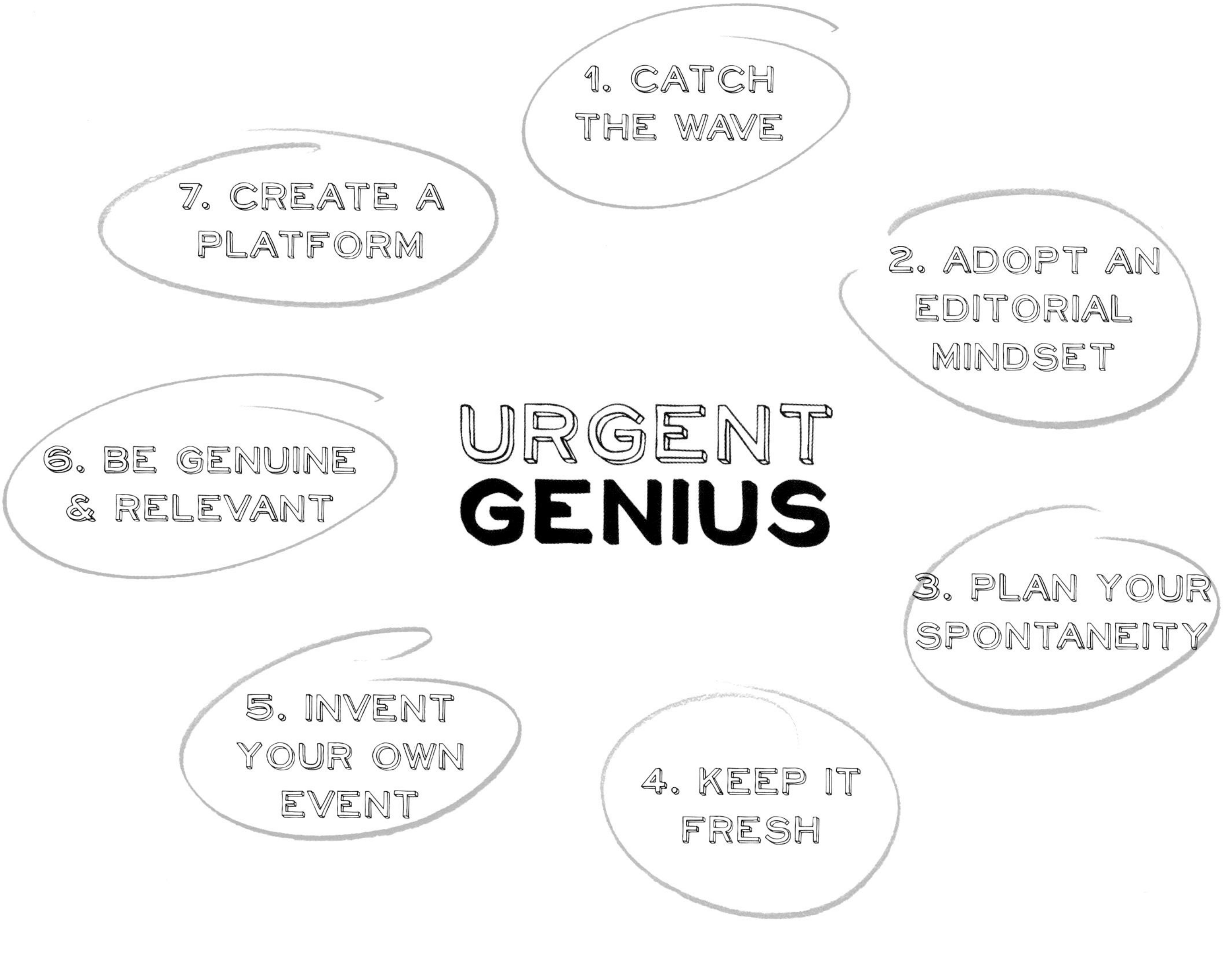

1. CATCH THE WAVE

7. CREATE A PLATFORM

2. ADOPT AN EDITORIAL MINDSET

URGENT GENIUS

6. BE GENUINE & RELEVANT

3. PLAN YOUR SPONTANEITY

5. INVENT YOUR OWN EVENT

4. KEEP IT FRESH

'...ideas are most likely to catch fire within 48 hours of the story breaking.'

David Meerman Scott

1. Catch the wave

The most obvious and important of our principles: is it trending? Fashionable is not enough – has it made the news? Is it the most read? Most emailed? Most searched-for? Does it ride the wave of a current trend?

A digitally enabled world means that news shifts faster; readers are already bored with news not yet in the papers. Stories have a shorter shelf life to accommodate our shorter attention spans. Conversely, this means our brains are more cluttered than ever, so a story had better be memorable to make it stand out.

In his book *Real-time Marketing and PR*, David Meerman Scott maintains that ideas are most likely to catch fire within forty-eight hours of the story breaking. This is called the Real-time Power Law and with this in mind, you must strike while the iron is hot. You must be prepared to ride out the popularity of a story, resigned to the knowledge that any reward for

your efforts may be short-lived. That's what this is all about. Try it. Experience the thrill of an instant success. Or fail fast and move on.

This chapter takes a detailed look at a range of creative responses to those stories that spread like wildfire. It also considers the balance of Urgent and Genius. Ideas that catch aren't always the best or the most carefully planned, but thanks to a combination of humour, invention and perfect timing, they instantly capture the public imagination. Some of our examples ride the wave of breaking news. Others are slow burners. What they have in common, however, is timing – the belief that one must strike now for maximum impact.

We start off with a bit of Urgent Genius that's been happening for almost a decade – a group of guys in London who ply their newsjacking trade on a cotton canvas.

2SickBastards is an independent T-shirt label based in London (see page 26). For the last nine years, they've made it their business to be first off the press (the screenprinting one) with topical T-shirts. They credit their success to acting as quickly as possible and choosing their subjects wisely. Designs include Kate Moss with a can of Coke, Michael Jackson Rest in Pieces as a police photo fit and Charlie Sheen as a high-stakes roller.

What prompted the creation of 2SB?

'We started 2SB in 2003 as an antidote to our commercial design jobs. We had some strong design ideas based on what was happening in the world. When the United States invaded Iraq we created our George 4 Saddam design, which we stencilled around London. That became the catalyst to start 2SB due to the response it received.'

How quickly do you go from a breaking news story to design and then production?

'It depends on the complexity of the concept, design and execution. Most of our designs take a certain amount of time to get absolutely right. Rest In Pieces was in stores within four weeks of Michael Jackson being administered a lethal injection by his doctor. We now sell all our designs online, which enables us to put them out there more quickly.'

Which design has been most successful, and do certain designs have a shelf life?

'Enjoy Kate is our most successful design. We were the first to put out a Kate Moss cocaine scandal design, which was huge news in the UK and fashion world. It's been copied many times since and still is. Our Britney Tears design was created when she had her meltdown. She then came back and that made the design irrelevant.'

'The essence of courage is timing. Take me, for example. I'll show up to fight anybody, anywhere. I'll just show up a day late.'

Jarod Kintz, $3.33

THE LIGHTNING FLASH OF MAGIC

Jon's mentor at VCU Brandcenter (Adcenter back then), Jelly Helm, said one thing to him in grad school that's always stuck with him. It's in the back of his mind everywhere he goes. He said: 'Jon, you're not telling anyone anything new, ever. You're just telling them something they already know and can relate to, but in a way they would never have thought before.' Author Neil Gaiman calls this a 'lightning flash of magic', and he looks for it in every story he reads. We call it Urgent Genius and we look for it in real-time creativity for brands and individuals.

So, we need to tell them something they can relate to. That sounds and smells like the word 'relevance' to us. So how do we know what they're thinking? How do we know what they're into? Enter stage left, social-media channels like Twitter and Facebook. People are volunteering this type of information every day. So if we time it just right, and enter a conversation that people are already having (that's the Urgent bit) with relevant targeted content that gets their attention (the Genius bit), they'll be more likely to appreciate it. How do you get their attention? Do something Genius and innovative that mixes old things up in a new way. It will hopefully

resonate with them and they'll pass it along to their friends as a sample of something that represents them and their sensibility.

One of our favourite authors, Rohit Bhargava, says it this way in his book *Likeonomics*:

'When it comes to timing, having a built-in sense of urgency is crucial because it lets people know that something is important in the moment when you are trying to influence them to care.
1. Necessary urgency: The first element in getting timing right is having a built-in sense of urgency so it is clear that someone needs to act or pay attention in the moment that matters.
2. Habitual connection: The best timing will connect your message or idea to a habit that the people you are trying to influence already have.
3. Current events: There are plenty of external factors that can influence getting timing right, so linking something to current events can only help with relevance.'

Yep, that's it. What Rohit said:
Urgency + Timing + Relevance (+ Creativity) = Urgent Genius.

Max Rietbergen,
SuperSocial, 2 Aug 2011

Facebook debuted a new look, with added photos at the top of the screen, at the end of 2010. Three weeks later, Schweppes and agency SuperSocial were quick to respond with their own Facebook hack, an app entitled Profile Yourself (see page 35). It allowed users to make one photo into a complete set, which spread across the new window layout at the top of a page.

Where did the idea SuperSocial come from?

'After Facebook launched the new profile page layout, creatives and innovators all around the world started experimenting with this new layout. French artist Andre Oudin took advantage of the new design to express himself. The creative uses went viral, and SuperSocial noticed the trend. People use Facebook to express themselves, but we noticed that it takes serious Photoshop skills to get it right. This inspired us to develop the Schweppes Profile App.'

THE LATEST HYPE ON FACEBOOK!
CREATE YOUR OWN UNIQUE PROFILE PAGE LAYOUT

content (see page 36). Created in Finland in February 2011, the platform works like an online photo gallery with a difference – it links photographers to the media, and enables them to put a price on their own work. Journalists can search by timeline, place or theme. The app allows freelance photographers to showcase their work, but it also speeds up the process of sourcing material, bringing print media that much closer to real time.

What was the time frame between Facebook launching the new profile and your app coming out?

'We almost immediately pitched the idea to Schweppes; they were very enthusiastic and gave approval for development. Facebook officially launched the new profile layout around 5 December 2010. The Schweppes Profile app was launched on 24 December. We received a lot of attention because we spotted the trend and were the first.'

How did Scoopshot come about?

'During the summer of 2009, I [Petri Rahja] acquired an iPhone and was thinking what else could be done with it. I started to monitor the usage of 'reader photos' in the media in Finland and the United States. A famous case in the industry is the emergency landing of the U.S. Airways flight on the Hudson River – an amateur photographer got to the scene, shot a photo with his phone and sent it to Twitpic. Twitpic own all the rights to photos people send to them. The photographer received very little (around \$50) compared to what Twitpic got (more than \$3,000,000).'

WATCH ▶

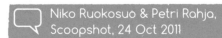
Niko Ruokosuo & Petri Rahja,
Scoopshot, 24 Oct 2011

Nothing is more shareable than a timely photo of a breaking news story. But who gets credit for the photos?

Scoopshot takes social media where few will dare to venture – it monetizes crowd-sourced

'If the focus of relevance is getting someone to care right now, the value of having the right timing is that it can help to make it urgent.'

Rohit Bhargava, *Likeonomics*

How has Scoopshot impacted on news reporting and the media?

'In a sense, when news reporting becomes fast, almost instant, it is then by definition real. There is no time to put a spin on it. It's simple, straightforward reporting.'

How efficient is Scoopshot?

'Scoopshot is a live stream of photos. All photos are no older than forty-eight hours. New photos are added to the system instantly when the 'Scoopshooters' take them. Typically media buy and publish the photo within minutes.'

'Your best work involves timing. If someone wrote the best hip-hop song of all time in the Middle Ages, he had bad timing.'

Scott Adams

standing dictator and 2011 was the year for fallen dictators, so the agency pondered with whom he would like to share his meal. They created an integrated campaign featuring a television ad, a twitter comp #mealfor6 and Mugabe look-a-likes delivering press kits to influential bloggers. The film shows Mugabe dreaming about the good times he had with his fallen comrades. From creating sand angels in the desert with Saddam Hussein to shooting water pistols with Muammar Gaddafi, the satirical wit of the campaign makes its point loud and clear – no one should eat alone thanks to Nando's.

Not everyone saw the funny side, and the campaign caused tensions to rise in neighbouring Zimbabwe as Mugabe's government caught wind of it. BBC World Africa reported on 2 December that Nando's employees in Zimbabwe had been threatened, and the company withdrew the ad for the safety of its staff. But the work had already

Ahmed Tilly
Black River FC, 10 July 2012

In South Africa, Black River FC were tasked by Nando's to create a festive-season campaign that would create talkability around their seasonal meals that are 'made for sharing' (see page 39). South Africans know Nando's for its irreverent advertising, so the agency tapped into a topical theme: Robert Mugabe is Southern Africa's last

gone viral and the rest of the world had embraced it. We talked to the ECD of Black River FC to find out more.

How did you come up with the idea for the Nando's campaign?

'As a brand, Nando's is known to be a social commentator. In 2011, Nando's asked us to develop a campaign for the year-end promotion. Our brief: develop a typically Nando's campaign that promotes a meal for six. Being near the end of the year, we started by looking at hot topics in the news arena. One team in particular realized that 2011 was the year that saw the fall of several dictators. This felt like an opportunity not to be missed.'

Can you talk about the approval process? Was the client nervous about the idea?

'At Black River FC, we do several reviews before presenting to our client. Several concepts were presented before the "Dictators" idea came about.

On the final presentation, two campaigns were presented: "Dictators" and a softer idea. There was some initial uncertainty when the idea was presented; in fact, I believe the client was split on the decision to go with the final idea. However, the client is usually encouraged by an idea that makes them a little uncomfortable, and therefore the "Dictators" idea survived the scrutiny of our client.'

What kind of reaction did the film get when it was released online?

'91,000 YouTube hits in twenty-four hours. The campaign trended on Twitter the day of the launch. Within eight weeks it had risen to two million total views, was featured in every major

'Without a sense of urgency, people won't give that extra effort that is often essential.'

John Kotter, Harvard Professor, *Leading Change*

THE SETTING FOR URGENT GENIUS

Urgent Genius started out as just a selfish way to keep boredom at bay in our day jobs. We've got short attention spans, both of us. Jon may even have an undiagnosed medical condition that only Twitter could cure – temporarily.

We're both impatient. We just want to get out there and do stuff. Grant was involved in one of the most long and drawn-out (albeit very rewarding) processes ever: creating London 2012 Olympic and Paralympic mascots Wenlock and Mandeville. It took over two years from brief to final decision. Jon was involved in a television shoot that took one-and-a-half years, which left him bored and dehydrated in the Spanish desert. To this day, he still gets dehydration headaches to remind him that he should be doing something more urgent with more chances of genius coming out of it.

We've always made stuff in our spare time – including award-winning short films – but it always leaves us wishing we could turn these quick-fire weekend competitions into a day job.

Then Twitter came along a few years later and we became obsessed with social media, insofar as it gave us a platform to launch content in a timely fashion. We want it right now. Fortunately so do other people. Then one day as we were fine-tuning the principles for Urgent Genius, in July 2009, we found out about a tired brand that had breathed life into their new shower gel by making 148 films in thirty-six hours. Thanks, Old Spice man, for inspiring us to keep pushing clients to do it now and over-think later.

'I have been impressed with the urgency of doing. Knowing is not enough; we must apply. Being willing is not enough; we must do. Without a sense of urgency, desire loses its value.'

Leonardo da Vinci

publication in the world – local, international, print and online – and even had a tweet from Stephen Fry!'

What did you learn from the process?

'Scrutiny of an idea is a good thing, but never spend too much time developing something. We had a very short space of time to get this ad from a blank page to completion. This meant quick decisions had to be made. It also meant that we didn't have time to over-analyse the concept. We didn't research it. We never research our ads. And discomfort is a good thing. We also learnt how important it is to have all players collaborating: agency, director, PR, social media, client, digital...all partners worked very closely together to get the job done.'

Catch the wave: It's all about timing. Choosing the right moment to strike with something that's hot right now but forgotten tomorrow. Let's get you started with a rather varied set of case studies that set the tone for this little tome.

1

Kit Kat
Longest Match

 Nestlé

JWT London

UK

June 2010

70-68

If you're into sport, here's your dream newsjacking brief: the longest match in the history of Wimbledon. As *USA Today* pointed out, in the 11 hours, 5 minutes it took John Isner to overcome Nicolas Mahut, you could have watched the rom-com *Wimbledon* 6.8 times. Why waste time with a sub-par film when you could shoot an ad, get client sign-off and arrange for ad-bikes to travel around the grounds displaying your Urgent Genius poster during that time? A perfect fit with the chocolate bar's 'Have a break' positioning, this ad is a brilliant example of the Urgent Genius mindset at work – everyone putting their day jobs on hold to make something brilliant happen. Bonus points if it involves an epic moment in sporting history.

Have a break. Have a

The ad was ready to go – they just had to wait for the match to end.

2SickBastards

 2SickBastards

 2SickBastards

 UK

2003 – present

London designers 2SickBastards have owned the poly-cotton newsjacking space for over a decade. Their T-shirt designs serve up a delightfully scathing view of modern pop culture. One of their first hits was their George Bush French-kissing Saddam Hussein design in 2003. Eight years later, it surely inspired Benetton to create their equally controversial Unhate campaign featuring several pairs of lip-locked leaders. While their designs aren't produced overnight, the celeb stories they hijack have a timeless quality to them. To our Urgent Genius-tuned ears, this sounds like a winning formula, especially if you fancy wearing a Charlie Sheen fruit machine across your chest.

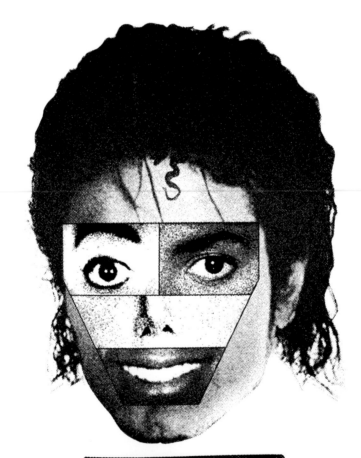

LOS ANGELES CA
DOA 25 06 09
REST IN PIECES
2SB

'We had some strong ideas based on what was happening in the world.'

Ben Aldis, 2SickBastards

Synergy
Chalkboards

 Synergy Fitness Club

 Joe D'Allegro

USA

2008 – present

'Stomp Mel Gibson's face…just $40 a month!' Synergy Fitness Club's advertising budget was the price of a stick of chalk, literally, but that tiny budget didn't stop them from getting worldwide acclaim. In fact, it helped. With sharp headline writing from part-time staffer Joe D'Allegro enticing passers-by, Synergy soon endeared themselves to the world by engaging an Urgent Genius mindset. Joe finds new headlines every week – including a British man who married a Russian spy and revealing that she had held secret meetings with her 'Russian friends' (bottom left), and U.S. politician Anthony Weiner's sexually explicit text messages (bottom right) and updates the board. This is the cheapest topical platform in this book by far, and we love it. The world's press also loved the topical attitude this small gym took up, giving them plenty of free coverage.

The fresher the story, the greater the impact.

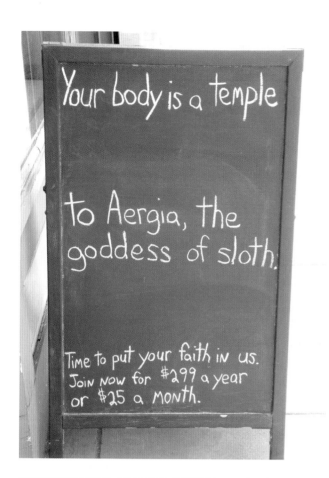

Your body is a temple

to Aergia, the goddess of sloth.

Time to put your faith in us. Join now for $299 a year or $25 a month.

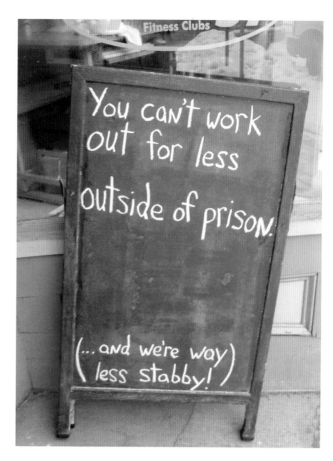

You can't work out for less outside of prison.

(...and we're way less stabby!)

Top secret Russian spy meeting spot ← (shhhh)

The passphrase is "Join now for only $40 a month."

Sexting women all across the country?

Better be ripped.

Join now for $25 a month.

PUMA Index

 PUMA Index

 Droga5 New York

 USA

 September 2009

The models stripped their way through the market meltdown.

After one of the biggest economic meltdowns in human history, experts worried that Wall Street wouldn't recover. Three scantily clad female models and one half-naked male model proved them wrong almost immediately thanks to Droga5 and the PUMA Index, an app that showed the models, each representing a different financial market, stripping down with every market drop. This stock-ticker app was a clever way to take real-time information and transform doom and gloom into something a bit more positive and playful. And more importantly, it got the traders spending as the app offered a 20 per cent discount on PUMA goods with the message: 'When the markets go down, the models' clothes come off.'

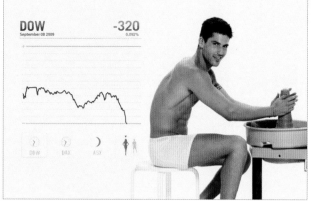

DOW   -320
September 08 2009   0.092%

DOW   DAX   ASX

EUROPE
THE DAX

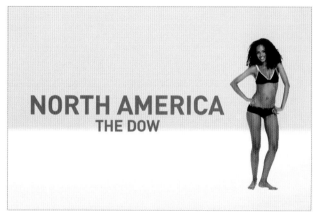

NORTH AMERICA
THE DOW

ASX 200   -250
September 08 2009   0.092%

DOW   DAX   ASX

Polo Snow Stamp

 Nestlé

 JWT London

 UK

 December 2009

Problem: A snowstorm brought London to a standstill. Solution: Use this act of nature as a genius opportunity for some clever branding. Tool: A modified rubbish bin lid, of course. JWT created a snow stamp to make a Polo imprint on the pure white of the freshly fallen snow, illustrating the nature of the mint perfectly. Instant and inspired, this bit of weatherjacking brought smiles to faces, bodies to corner shops and mints to pockets as London was dotted with these little Urgent gems of Genius within hours.

Snow mints appeared across London in a matter of hours.

Wikileaks...
Butterfly Doesn't

 Butterfly sanitary towels

 RG Blue Communications Karachi

 Pakistan

 December 2010

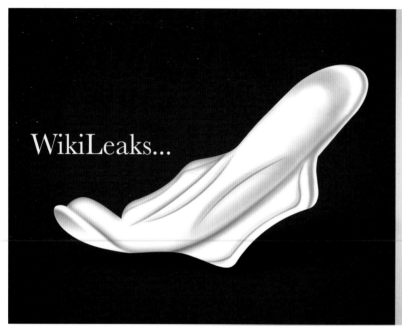

Oh look, a controversial espionage case in the United States – let's use it to sell sanitary napkins in Pakistan. As thousands of U.S. embassy documents were leaking onto Wikipedia, Karachi agency RG Blue piggybacked the scandal to create buzz for their unlikely yet tactical newsjacker – female hygiene brand Butterfly. This simple-yet-clever ad ran, sending a collective snigger across the web. Of course, many responses were: 'How did they get away with that in Pakistan?' For us, this bit of Urgent Genius was all about pushing a wild idea through without overthinking it. So what if the next brief you get is of a sensitive nature? Look to partner it with a nice topical scandal, perhaps?

> 'We had reservations that it wouldn't fly...but every other idea paled against it.'
>
> Munir Bhatti, Art Director, RG Blue Communications Karachi

Schweppes Profile App

Schweppes

SuperSocial

Netherlands

December 2010

One day in 2010, Mark Zuckerberg woke up and decided to give everyone a makeover. Facebook's new look added multiple photos to the top of the screen, and if you were handy with Photoshop you could manipulate this space in beautiful ways. However, many people were perfectly happy with the old look and objected to Zuckerberg's meddling. Schweppes teamed up with Dutch agency SuperSocial to create the Profile app, which allowed people to easily spread one photo across the new layout. The app rode the wave of Facebook's newsworthy changes with a brand app that was actually useful, and Schweppes let everyone live happily ever after…until the next makeover.

Schweppes and SuperSocial democratized creativity.

Scoopshot

 Scoopshot

N Ruokosuo and P Rahja

Finland

February 2011 – present

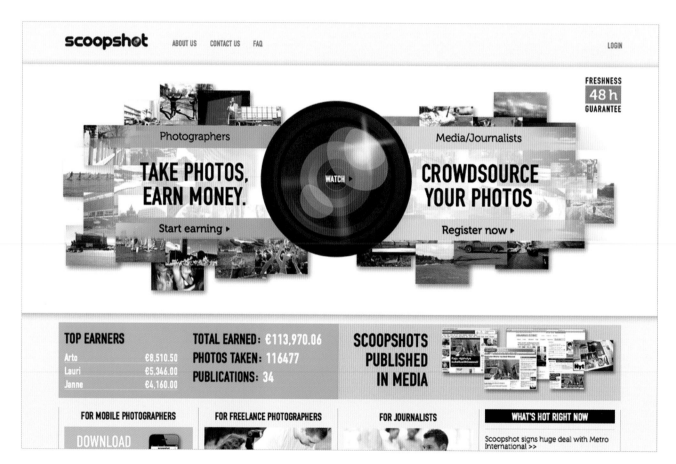

Elevator pitch: If a photographer's pics are 'right place, right time' then she deserves the 'right money, right now'. While marketing's big brains were pondering how to monetize crowd-sourced content, Scoopshot swooped in with answers. Created in Finland in early 2011, the app gave the online photo gallery a good ol' 21st-century shake down. Anyone can put a price tag on their favourite snaps and get them under the nose of hungry journos in seconds as they search by timeline, place or theme.

It speeds up the process of sourcing material.

It's the debt crisis. The United States needs cash. Solution: A detergent brand chips away at the debt by slipping Obama $25 million to rename the country's most famous house the 'Vanish NapiSan White House'? This tongue-in-cheek offer included a personal video to the U.S. President and an extensive effort to lobby government officials. The campaign generated 15 times more media coverage than any previous effort, which came in handy when the laundry brand launched the real campaign 'keeping white clothes white' and sponsored a real Aussie family who lived in a large white house. This cheeky multi-platform campaign made Vanish NapiSan totally relevant and top-of-mind with consumers.

White House Sponsorship

 Vanish NapiSan

 Euro RSCG Sydney

 Australia

 July 2011

'Obama, we'll sponsor the White House for $25 million.'

Steve Jobs RIP

 Self-promotion

 Jonathan Mak

Hong Kong

October 2011

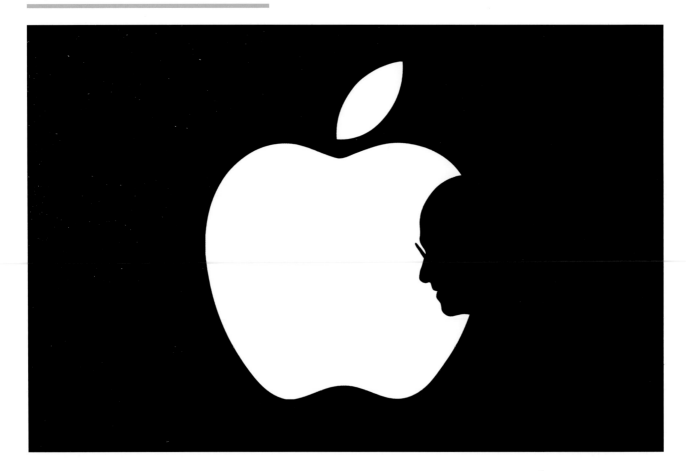

Newsflash: 'Apple creates new logo. It appears online and no one notices.' Okay, this would never happen, but it could have happened thanks to nineteen-year-old Jonathan Mak and his Premature Genius. The day Apple's tech-saint resigned, he put his brilliant logo on Tumblr, and it barely caused a ripple. So he reposted it moments after Apple's former CEO passed away, and it went viral within hours. In fact, it was the most shared image online for what was Twitter's biggest ever spike. Mak embraced the newsjacking mindset of just 'think, make, launch' and his career took off. Lesson learned: timing is everything. Get it wrong the first time and just wait for another trigger. It might catapult you from student to superstar overnight.

The graphic lay unnoticed until the announcement of Jobs' passing away on the fifth.

Nando's Last Dictator Standing

 Nando's

 Black River FC

 South Africa

November 2011

Nando's believe their meals are 'made for sharing'. So yes, Africa's last standing dictator Robert Mugabe, that means you. To prove he still had friends, ad agency Black River FC created this satirical film showing him reminiscing about the fun times he had with his lost comrades. It linked to a promotion that asked the public to nominate the six friends they'd most like to have dinner with, and it quickly went viral. Nando's had shown how to strike gold by relating a topical story to the brand and taking it to a satirical, playful extreme.

'Two million YouTube views is way more satisfying than a statue from any awards show.'

Ahmed Tilly, Black River FC

'As a news organisation we know that the internet is a conversation...being relevant is key.'

Micheal Logan – Head of content, NMA

2. Adopt an editorial mindset

Traditional ad-agency methods and structures have remained largely static since the *Mad Men* era, minus the extreme sexism, incessant smoke-athons and entire departments of typists. However, in recent years, visionaries at digital agencies have shaken things up more than ever before with a hybrid approach to creativity. Urgent Genius requires this stepped change, both in how agencies operate internally and how they interact with their clients. To react to breaking news in a timely manner, agencies must both create and self-edit, producing content at a moment's notice before an avalanche of rival media drowns out their voice.

Of course, this means that traditional, focused roles are no longer relevant. The most prized skill is an alert and open mind. Art directors and copywriters become less important when everyone is their own producer and creative-in-chief. Agencies are evolving to become more like newsrooms, creating a new hybrid of 'brand journalism' and working to news-like deadlines.

In this chapter we'll explore what it takes to develop an editorial mindset. We'll examine real-time documentaries, BAFTA-nominated dramas and CGI animations created in a matter of hours. In a nutshell, we'll explain how hybrid thinking is key to creating Urgent Genius.

Our look at the editorial mindset kicks off with a whodunnit soap opera that drip-fed storylines across multiple platforms. A drama set across social-media platforms, *Who Killed Summer* (see page 50) was an early innovator before 'transmedia' became a well-worn buzzword. Unlike ordinary campaigns, the creative team was challenged to craft a story that would unfold in real time and last the summer months. It was advertising bordering on film-making for entertainment. The campaign also required a keen eye on social media. Originally conceived around MySpace and Bebo, it rapidly migrated to Facebook where the real interaction took place.

Richard Welsh, Bigballs,
15 April 2011

What was it like working in real-time and on a never-ending deadline?

'It very nearly killed us all! I lost count of the number of days we were in the office past 2 a.m. sorting out translation issues or tweaking storylines – or on the road with a broken-down bus, trying to find a decent upload link to send files back to the edit.'

What were the different skills that you needed to make the campaign work?

'The project was a real mix of talent: film and television production, Bigballs' fast turnaround experience, agency folk helping manage the brand, digital producers, social-media people…everyone doing a bit of everyone else's jobs. It was a perfect example of how one company should include all of this experience, and that the walled garden approach of "marketing", "television" and "brands" etc. is over.'

Do you think the future of creative work is real time?

'Staying still is what kills projects – if you want to stand out, decide to do something that you have no idea how to achieve…you'll work it out…the real opportunity with web storytelling is to use real time – something that television can never replicate.'

'Too much time standing in one place is bad for your corporate health. Drive, run, or walk to your customers with technology, information, and personalized service.'

Tom Kelley, *Ten Faces of Innovation*

 Sarah Rich, Longshot,
17 April 2011

The guys at *Longshot* crafted a traditional-format magazine in record time, while simultaneously proving that rumours of the format's death are greatly exaggerated. *Longshot* magazine (see page 51) was conceived one evening when the founders were talking about the future of publishing and looking at a magazine that had been produced using

FROM REAL-TIME TO NEWSROOM

In the early days of Urgent Genius, the examples in this chapter were what we dreamed about. This was back when we thought our careers would always be a painful, drawn-out meeting where people discuss how they can slowly crucify our ideas, soul and spirit. A bit dramatic, yes, but the truth remains: the people who convinced their clients to let them create content in real time and get it out there within minutes – they are living the dream. 99 per cent of clients couldn't cope with this a year or so ago. Now, they're having to do it. They're still overworked. They just have had to trust agency folk a lot more – plus the collaboration teams have grown larger so there are more people to share the real-time blame when it all goes wrong.

The ideas in this chapter are all about doing it quickly. The editorial mindset is: who what when where and get it out there fast. Craft quickly, and fine-tune your skills so you can make it as good as you can, as quickly as you can.

This is about speed. So go on, set yourself up as a newsroom. Google Gatorade Mission Control, Golin Harris or sparks & honey, a company that co-author Jon had the pleasure of working with in New York. By the time you're reading this there may be hundreds of agencies with newsrooms. Let's hope so.

the print-on-demand service MagCloud. The *Longshot* team wanted to experiment, but without tying people into a long-term project, so they set themselves the challenge to create a forty-eight-hour magazine.'

How did the idea form?

'We wanted to experiment with the possibilities of print-on-demand through a project that would not demand too much of anyone's time, given we all worked full-time, so that was the original motivation for doing it in forty-eight hours (over a weekend).'

What are the main challenges of working to a forty-eight-hour schedule?

'Sleep deprivation, for one. Also the need to be sure we have a very tight editorial-management system for fielding submissions so nothing falls through the cracks. For the designers,

the forty-eight-hour period is definitely a challenge, simply because taking a full magazine layout from concept to execution generally takes a lot more time. And finally, proofing things when you've been up for forty-eight hours is tough, but for that we bring in a special copy editor, so that we have at least one attentive, sharp set of eyes on the entire magazine before it ships.'

Anything that's surprised you in the process?

'I'd say the one big thing I've taken away from this is that while the process and the project itself hinge largely on web-based tools and there's quite a bit of remote collaboration going on, it's nevertheless invaluable to have face-to-face, on-site work for the actual editing, design and production. Being together in one place allows for spontaneous creative decisions and it also creates a really significant bond and sense of accomplishment.'

Dan Brooks, 180 Amsterdam,
6 April 2010

During the 2010 Football World Cup in South Africa, 180 Amsterdam adopted an editorial approach on their work for adidas (see page 54). Dan Brooks wore two hats as both creative and director, writing and shooting the documentaries as he went along. It was a brave move on adidas' part, banking on content that had to be shot and cleared in a day.

How did the creation and execution of this project differ from usual?

'The process was simple but had to be very immediate: come up with an idea, go shoot it, whizz back to edit, have it done by the late evening, get it all cleared by legal and client, and ready for the following morning. It was all about momentum and relevance – if the moment was missed, the work lost its significance. Everything was time critical.'

How did you prepare?

'Prior to going, we had drawn up a plan for the thirty-two days, the key dates, anticipated moments to react on, but it wasn't long before I had to orchestrate instinctively around [the plan]. So I think the process was much more spontaneously creative, with no time to tweak or fiddle, chop, change or meddle, and that helped make the work appear more honest, not so contrived or too "advertising-y"!'

How did it differ from a traditional adidas advertising campaign?

'One reason it differed from any other previous adidas campaign was that Facebook and YouTube were the primary broadcast channels. We had built a following of well over one million in a really short time on adidas Facebook. The number of fans kept growing the more content we seeded.'

What challenges did you face along the way?

'The main challenge I faced as a creative was having limited resources in a very unfamiliar, sprawling African city, and having to find solutions to it in a very short time. For example, we street cast, so we would go up to fans and ask if they would donate themselves for little more than a few beers. We were arrested for lighting distress flares on the beach in Durban, filmed in the roughest neighbourhoods with people coming up to us all the time, but without all the risks we might never have produced the work we did.'

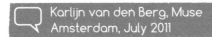
Karlijn van den Berg, Muse
Amsterdam, July 2011

Editorial thinking continues with a sort of dial-a-journalist service: reporters on demand giving consumers their personal news wire.

SuperSwypers was created for Samsung by Starcom and Muse Amsterdam (see page 56). A crack team of roving personal reporters, the SuperSwypers spent the summer recording events and festivals for those who couldn't attend. Users could enlist them to check into foursquare, shoot videos and photos, and use the Swype feature on the Galaxy S to ensure they covered every minute of action. The results were then edited into a custom video that could be viewed online.

Interesting idea, how did you come up with it?

'Swype is the fastest way of inputting text and the most distinctive feature on the Galaxy S, so we came up with the concept of SuperSwypers:

the fastest journalists on earth. Samsung immediately loved the idea....They just gave us carte blanche on setting up a team, multiple social network accounts and working with young professionals. Looking back, it's quite special that Samsung had the guts to trust us on this.'

How big was the team working on it?

'The creative team was about six people: conceptors and designers. Development of the site was outsourced. We then used twenty young professionals in our team of SuperSwypers, who were prepped and coached by a team of three. The whole company worked really hard and we basically created a fully staffed temporary news department in our agency.'

Was it worth all the trouble?

'It was a rollercoaster ride, but we still have really nice memories from it. Creating services for brands instead of simple activations is where future communications and concepts opportunities are. Brands are always on, 365 days per year.'

'To think is easy. To act is difficult. To act as one thinks is the most difficult.'

Johann Wolfgang Von Goethe

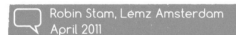
Robin Stam, Lemz Amsterdam
April 2011

The IKEA 365 campaign produced a new commercial every day to illustrate IKEA's motto, 'Every day different' (see page 62). In a truly Urgent Genius undertaking, a streamlined crew shot fifteen commercials in a day twice a month throughout the year, picking up on cultural trends. Robin Stam created the campaign with his Art Director partner Luiz Risi.

Where did the Ikea365 idea come from?

'We were in a pitch against three other agencies. To win, we needed to come up with something so different and so revolutionary that it would position us way above the competition from the start. My team partner Luiz and I once had the idea of making a new commercial every day for a few weeks. It was for a lottery and there wasn't enough budget to do such a thing. We didn't know whether it would be possible for IKEA, but as soon as this idea was there, we worked very hard to prove that we could do

it. We actually shot five different commercials within half a day, to show the client that was possible. And in the end we won the pitch.'

What were the challenges of shooting a new commercial every day?

'There was always time pressure. For every script there were at least three rejected ones, which meant that to shoot fourteen commercials you have to write around sixty commercials. Sometimes we had to come up with a new script one hour before deadline. The agency had meetings with the client every day. We were very disciplined and every two weeks we would shoot fourteen or fifteen new commercials.'

Any funny stories from the process?

'If you make so many commercials, there's always a shortage of actors. Especially when you have to hire a specific character. I once wrote a script about a creative in trendy pants and with long hair. My creative director told me: "Hey, why don't you play the creative yourself?" A few weeks later I was on the set, playing myself!'

'The new source of power is not money in the hands of a few, but information in the hands of many.'

John Naisbitt

Michael Logan, NMA
April 2011

Next Media Animation is a team of animators who turn around CGI re-enactments of news incidents within hours of their taking place (see page 49). Everyone from Miley Cyrus to Al Gore has been the target of NMA humour, the idea being that a 'cartoonified' version of the news is more compelling, and gives us the chance to see retrospective events as they happened. Their animation of the downfall of Tiger Woods, produced hours after the breaking news, garnered over six million views. Speed of response has been a massive factor in terms of growing a global audience. NMA has a three-hour production cycle, although when they really need to they can go to final CGI animation in just an hour and a half.'

How do you manage to respond to breaking news so quickly?

'Over a two-year period we invested heavily in R&D and built a massive database of CGI models and environments. We have tens of thousands of models on tap, which we can customize pretty much instantly. As a news organization, we know that the internet is a conversation…being relevant is key.'

What does the team for this project look like?

'The teams working on a project can be up to two dozen people, including storyboard artists, motion-capture animators and music composers, watched over by journalism-style editors who get the final say. There are no set editorial meetings at NMA, it's much more organic. We are all just news junkies!'

The editorial mindset: companies, agencies, individuals across the globe with rapid-fire responses. Shedding cumbersome agency structures and processes, they can sit at the cutting edge. This mindset is the incubator for entirely new and exciting creative possibilities.

The case studies on the next few pages show highlights of these amazing international successes. Grab a cuppa, have a read and let the inspiration sink in: it's your turn next.

2

Next Media Animation

 Next Media Animation

 Next Media Animation

 Taiwan

2009 – present

CNN on steroids meets Jon Stewart's *The Daily Show* in the style of Grand Theft Auto. That's how a Hollywood producer would sell in Next Media Animation. The script: Animation studio invests heavily in motion-capture technology to create a library of tens of thousands of CGI models. Production: They make up to thirty satirical animations a day, releasing videos within hours of a story breaking. Marketing: They shot to international attention by depicting Tiger Woods' spurned wife as a golf-club-wielding crazy lady and pitting Steve 'Darth Vader' Jobs in a lightsaber fight with Bill Gates (see right). Box-office results: Their YouTube channel boasts around 4.1 million daily hits, and the company makes about $210 million a year in revenue.

From storyboard to full CGI animation in just 90 minutes.

Who Killed Summer?

 Vodafone

 Bigballs London

 UK

2009

Imagine if your favourite soap opera traded television for Facebook. That's what Vodafone's BAFTA-nominated murder mystery *Who Killed Summer?* essentially did. With six main characters, they toured some of Europe's greatest music festivals, from Benicàssim to Global Gathering. Each of the twenty episodes interacted in real time via direct messages, status updates and video content, with over five million fans over nine weeks. This was an ambitious experiment in content production. By delivering a new chapter every 48 hours, the client, Vodafone, had just one day to approve the work. The kids wanted a revolution, and that's just what they got.

'Staying still is what kills projects...do something that TV can never replicate.'

Richard Welsh, Bigballs

Longshot

📢 *Longshot*

✍ *Longshot*

📍 USA

🕐 July 2009

Longshot: Your mission, should you chose to accept it, is to take the 'print-is-dead' crowd head-on by creating and producing a high-quality magazine from scratch in just forty-eight hours. Much like the Urgent Genius Weekender (see page 186), each issue's theme is set on a Friday night, just as most creators are getting their first drink in. The first issue, originally called *48HR*, centred on the theme 'HUSTLE' and attracted over 1,500 contributors, who sent in words, photos and drawings. Seventy articles were then chosen, printed and shipped.

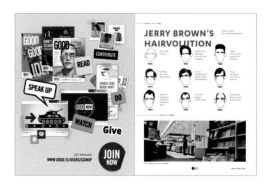

Forty-eight hours to create the future of publishing.

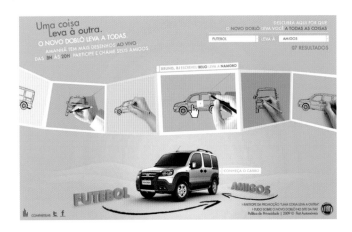

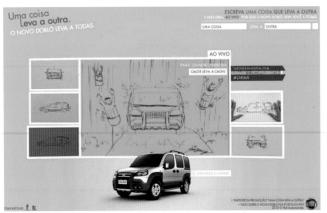

Fiat Novo Doblo

📢 Fiat Novo Doblo

✏️ Agencia Click

📍 Brazil

🕐 January 2010

Fiat drafted in a crack team of animators to bring consumers' imaginations to life on the small screen. Users were encouraged to dictate the Novo Doblo's journey by entering their idea into a simple scenario generator. Requests were then interwoven to create a lucid, real-time stream of consciousness, before being posted on Fiat's social-media accounts. Suggestions saw the family-friendly Fiat travelling through space, over mountains and even getting married. By illustrating their line, 'One thing leads to another' (in eight-hour shifts), Fiat were able to inject a healthy amount of Urgent Genius into the technique of user generation.

8,500 requests in five days.

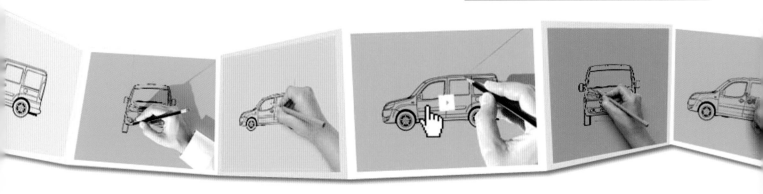

2010 World Cup

 adidas

 180 Amsterdam

 International

 April 2010

World Cup sponsor adidas gave a documentary crew their dream brief by sending them to South Africa for the 2010 World Cup. Telling them to capture the real lives of those living on the mean streets of this amazing country turned into a logistical nightmare, but made for fascinating viewing. Working around puny production times (shooting, cutting and uploading in a day), they set the internet alight by getting arrested on Durban beach, coming to the attention of local gang members and paying talent with beer alone, yet they managed to tell the tales of those living in the shadows of the World Cup in as close to real time as possible.

'The main challenge...few resources, in a very unfamiliar, sprawling city.'
Dan Brooks, Director

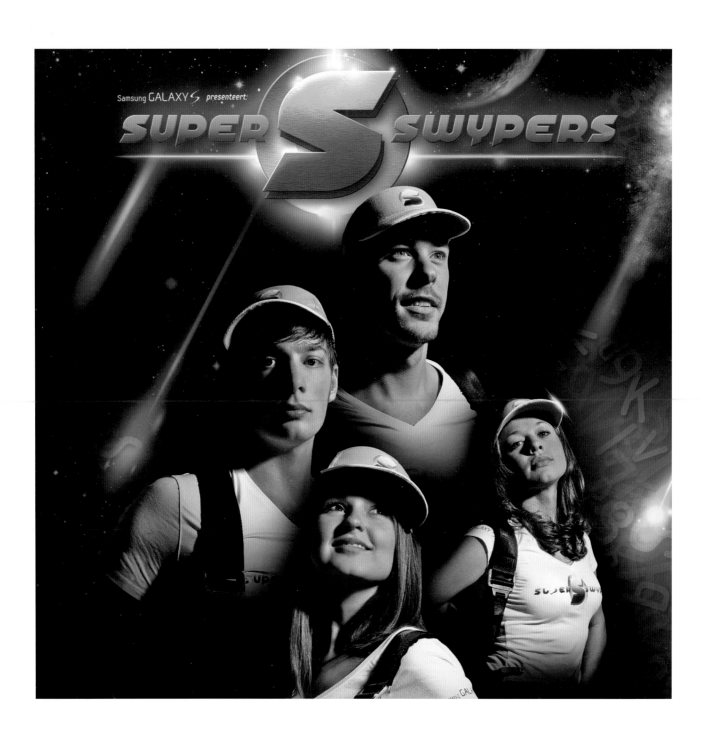

SuperSwypers

 Samsung

 Muse Amsterdam

 Netherlands

August 2010

Until scientists get it together and invent instant teleportation, there'll always be things we'll miss. Thankfully, Samsung took up the mantle with the SuperSwypers, a team of speed bloggers who attend all those events and festivals you can't. Using the Swype app (run your finger across the screen for 50 per cent faster typing) these bloggers gave the play-by-play via words, photos and videos, all published live via Twitter, Facebook and YouTube, meaning you're there in spirit, rather than person. The result: SuperSwypers were rushed to over 160 events, reaching 600,000 people.

The fastest journalists on earth.

Step Inside the Circuit

 Johnnie Walker

 iris worldwide Singapore and Firecracker Films

 International

 March 2011 – present

Do you wanna watch the F1 from my suite at the Hotel de Paris or from my yacht? Johnnie Walker's 'Step Inside the Circuit' campaign, created by iris worldwide and Firecracker Films, gives a fascinating glimpse into the lives of Lewis Hamilton and Jenson Button. Through a mixture of in-depth interviews and documentary-style films – all shot, edited and uploaded within forty-eight hours – we see a world populated by the young and the beautiful, all pandered to by yacht brokers and property agents. This campaign informed and entertained with content so good that F1 broadcasters ran it as programming. Now if you don't mind, our caviar's getting warm.

'It's launch and learn in real time.'

Ewan Topping, Diageo

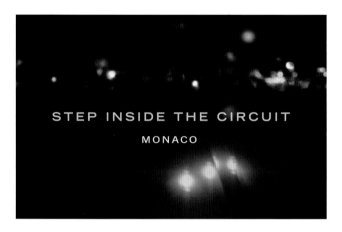

STEP INSIDE THE CIRCUIT
MONACO

MAY 2011
RACE WEEKEND
MONACO

THE YACHT BROKER

'The "*Dogme* approach"...limitations helped us.'
Roger Gual, Director

Hotel Casa Camper

 Camper

Boolab

Spain

March 2011

Recipe for disaster: Put six film directors in a crowded hotel and give them an extreme deadline. Hotel Casa Camper gave six completely different directors twenty-four hours to create six stories, which then had to be cut into one feature film. The final 'concoction' of six stories had everything in it -- comedy, drama and special effects, all set inside the intriguing world of Hotel Casa Camper. The end result had great reviews as well. An experiment we hope to emulate for our next Urgent Genius Weekender (see page 186). Any hotels in the Maldives up for it?

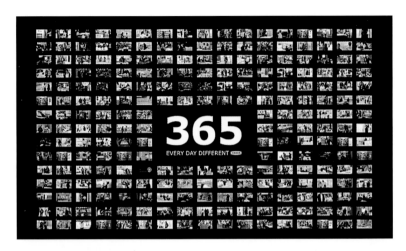

IKEA 365

 IKEA Netherlands

 Lemz

 Netherlands

🕐 January – December 2011

You've been there. New business pitch. It's make or break. If you're slightly unhinged like the guys at Lemz, you say: 'What about a new ad every day for a year?' Pushing the boundaries of advertising production, Lemz mixed topical content with scripted ads to shoot a mammoth 365 unique commercials. They shot fifteen ads a day twice a month, releasing the topical ones first, putting the editorial mindset to the test to devastating effect.

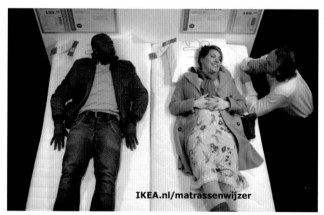

A new commercial every day for a year.

'We came up with the idea six months before the World Cup began.'

Bas & Dan, Wonderyears

3. Plan your spontaneity

Often preparation is as important as instinct. The geniuses we'll highlight in this chapter keep an ear fixed to the ground, listening out for the rumblings of upcoming news. They obsessively monitor trending topics and experiment often. This helps them fine-tune their sense of how long an event will stay hot for and whether it's worth pursuing.

Here's how 'planned spontaneity' works for us at Urgent Genius HQ: We keep track of upcoming events, launches, holidays, etc. – from Valentine's Day and April Fool's Day to the World Cup in Brazil and National Talk Like A Pirate Day. At present we are developing a beautiful data visualization tool that helps us with this process.

Then there are events that we know will happen sooner or later: Prince Harry will eventually settle down and attempt to throw another Royal Wedding. So we'd be wise to start planning a Ginger Prince Day and hope that the Queen cares enough to give us another holiday.

In this section, we feature ideas and products that turned familiar yearly events into creative gold. The most clichéd days are ripe for reinvention, whether it's enhancing the experience of the World Cup with personalization and technical innovation or providing an alternative to the cheesy Royal Wedding memorabilia. In each example, the brand has identified an event ideally suited to them and approached the task with varying degrees of irreverence.

WHAT IF YOUR CLIENT IS WORLDS AWAY FROM BEING URGENT OR GENIUS?

Planned spontaneity is the 'get-out clause' for those who can't wrap their heads around the Urgent bit. There are some things you can plan, which when they happen may seem incredibly spontaneous. This is Urgent Genius with stabilizers on. This is our way in with several clients. Urgent Genius is about doing stuff and launching it when the time is right. So let's take Christmas as an example of planned spontaneity.

It happens every year, right? Check. Perfect. And brands start preparing for it earlier and earlier. Our local corner shop in London already has mince pies out in September. So a mince-pie-related act of Urgent Genius may have missed the boat already. Okay, well, let's think about one of our favourite ideas in this chapter and we'll steal the case studies' thunder a bit. Now an agency in Portugal faced the same dreaded brief that every agency gives to the junior team now – the Christmas greeting to clients. This agency decided to tell the oldest story in the world in a completely new way using online platforms like Twitter, Amazon, Wikipedia, Farmville, etc. The planned spontaneity of it all comes in

their timing as they knew that their genius execution, which went viral globally, wouldn't get the traction it needed if it was launched too close to Christmas where it had to compete with an influx of holiday-themed stuff. So they launched it the day before a national holiday in Portugal – in early December. They banked on folks being at home and on YouTube on a holiday – a risk, as the 'bored office network' is often a major catalyst to shareability – but it paid off and it was perfect.

Not all the examples in this chapter fit in this neat little perfectly timed box. But what if your agency's not ready to turn on a dime? What if your client has no system in place? Wait, this is all good, but it will never work because our clients never, and never ever will, work this way. It's not hardwired in their DNA. Okay, we get that. So what about conversations that we already know are happening? Do something that's already on the calendar. What events can you hijack? Are there any preset norms in place that you could shatter?

 Stika, Monorex art collective, 16 August 2011

Amid the Royal Wedding buzz, there was opportunity to pass comment on the commentators. Monorex artist Stika created the oversized statement mural, reading 'Don't Hate on Kate', across a wall at the back of an arts centre in Shoreditch, London (see page 75).

Do you see street art as a more immediate platform for conveying a message?

'Public art – and street art in particular – is an incredible communication platform. With all of our trends, interests and conversations moving

so quickly, we need some sort of quick-fire art response, alongside the craziness.'

What was your message?

'It was our reaction to all the negative waffle in the press at the time and the negativity among

'Twenty years from now you will be more disappointed by the things that you didn't do than by the ones you did do. So throw off the bowlines. Sail away from the safe harbor. Catch the trade winds in your sails. Explore. Dream. Discover.'

Mark Twain

Frustrated by the official wedding plate's two-week waiting list, not to mention its sheer lack of imagination, Hoxton design shop KK Outlet recruited seven different artists to come up with a modern alternative (see page 77). The resulting designs were a sell out, featuring designs like Kate's wedding list (toaster, new tiara, Oxfordshire) and the message: 'THANKS FOR THE FREE DAY OFF'.

So, what was the aim of the project?

'The brief was kind of to design a Royal Wedding plate for the Facebook generation. We thought it'd be better to embrace the Royal Wedding and celebrate it, rather than be sarcastic. Things like "Give it six months" were too negative to make the cut.'

younger crowds who had absolutely no interest in the event, let alone an understanding of the monarchy. We maintained our cheeky edge with some of our prints like "Marry Harry" and "Keepin' It Royal".'

The Royal Wedding really consumed the news for several months leading up to the day itself. Did you see it as an issue that art could make a comment on?

'It was only while carrying out the project that we realized there were other street artists getting involved. We expected stuff from the usual current-affairs guys like Banksy, Shepard Fairey and Tristan Eaton, but didn't really gauge what was going on until the final days leading up to the wedding. Our decision was purely based on our opinion at the time; it was pretty much 90 per cent "let's have a laugh" and 10 per cent "maybe we should sell some prints online". I think it's really important to remember that most artists are still producing work to express themselves as opposed to knocking stuff out to impress others.'

How did you go about producing and promoting the plates?

'They were only meant as a window display. We just got one-offs made and had them on display in the gallery. Then people started taking photographs of them and they started showing up on blogs. Once journalists got hold of them, we started thinking we should probably put the plates into production.'

So is this a case of the product becoming viral before it had even gone on sale?

'Yes, I think we just nailed it and summed up what people were thinking.'

Football-mad students Bas van de Poel and Daan van Dam created a fan shirt for Holland that went the extra mile, with a star player's face printed inside that fans could show every time the team scored (see page 80).

First things first, how did the idea come about?

'We came up with the shirt idea during a school project. It was cool to combine our two biggest passions: football and creativity. We chose the most popular players in the Dutch squad at the time.'

Was the shirt planned far in advance?

'We came up with the shirt six months before the World Cup began. We sent images of the shirt to several friends and bloggers. After a couple of days, some well-known blogs started writing about it. From there it took flight. However, we weren't able to actually produce it after we received a letter from the Dutch Football Federation. They weren't cool with us using their players.'

Holland has an interesting history of design. Do you see more room for creativity in sports merchandise?

'It's quite difficult to realize sport merchandise ideas. Especially when you aren't working for a major sport brand.'

World Cup coverage took a surreal turn when Paul the Octopus made a series of result 'predictions' based on his feeding patterns. In a quick-fire campaign for Burger King Singapore, Publicis re-imagined Paul as a Chihuahua with comedy tentacles (see page 79). They set the dog loose on a collision course with different Burger King snacks in a series of YouTube videos. Using a specially created Facebook app, followers could bet which snacks Rebel the Octopuppy would go for. Winners of the 'snacking quick pick' were then sent Burger King vouchers in the post.

How did you come up with the idea for Octopuppy?

'Part of Burger King's strategy for marketing is to tap into pop culture and what's current. Leveraging interesting news and events happening during the promo will get the audience's attention and has more talk factor. That said, we knew it would be near impossible to control an octopus for a shoot, so our best alternative was to dress up something small to look like an octopus.'

How quickly did the idea go from concept to realization?

'We had no more than six weeks to come up with the idea, create a campaign strategy around it, produce it and launch it. Fortunately, they bought it instantly. This campaign hit the sweet spot in terms of what the brand stood for.'

Who is the puppy and did she/he have to be trained to sniff out the daily deals?

'The puppy's real name is Rebel and he belongs to a good friend of mine. He had no prior training at all and we had to tempt him with his favourite snack by placing them behind the props. This entire process had to be thought through the moment we came up with the idea.'

'The act of giving someone a smile, of connecting to a human, of taking initiative, of being surprising, of being creative, of putting on a show—these are things that we do for free all our lives. And then we get to work and we expect to merely do what we're told and get paid for it.'

Seth Godin *Linchpin*

Play BK Quick Pick or I will tickle you till you squeal like a little girl.

Reliably angry punks, Fucked Up have an online presence, using their blog to expose malpractice in the music industry. In April 2010 they stunned fans by revealing that a previous tirade had made them the subject of a lawsuit, originating with a little-known energy drinks brand called 'Thriller', with its own shady, oddly hyperbolic website (see page 86). The band petitioned fans for support, only to reveal soon afterwards on Canadian television station Much Music that the whole thing was a hoax.

What was your aim with the 'Thriller Energy Drinks' lawsuit prank?

'Every year we try to prank our fans with an April Fool's joke on our blog. We'd been getting a lot of internet attention in the months leading up to April 1st, so we knew that the prank would get a lot of coverage if we pulled it off well.'

How long in advance did you plan the whole thing?

'We literally had maybe one full day to put everything together. I was out of town when I came up with the idea, and emailed Josh from our band, who is a website programmer (and also my old room-mate). It was very rushed but we had a clear idea of what we needed to do to make it believable – just a blog post wasn't going to be enough because we've already got a reputation for telling lies and pulling pranks. The website was the centrepiece. We knew that people are web-savvy but also lazy.'

The fake lawsuit put web media in the firing line. Was that intentional, to expose just how easily unverified news can go global?

'Not really, but we ran with it once it took off. We got on live TV to talk about the lawsuit, there were countless stories on the internet, we did radio interviews, there was this big Facebook page we made in defence of the band. It really took off in just a few hours.'

'The biggest challenge for brands looking to keep pace with digital is to make the transition from saying to doing. So rather than sending out messages that say what the brand thinks they should be, they should instead create services and experiences that demonstrate what the brand is. That's the biggest transition that advertising needs to make—from message pushers to service providers.'

Akas Ahmed, AKQA founder and author of *Velocity*

I'M BACK!

Henning, Rogge & Pott,
12 September 2011

Design company Rogge & Pott of Hamburg
played a prank at the expense of the notoriously
po-faced photography community by claiming
to launch a new and innovative product,
the Re35, which allegedly combined digital
photography with traditional 35mm film.
The buzz was instant, both when eager SLR
fans swarmed the site looking to buy one, and
again when it was revealed to be a cleverly
contrived hoax.

So how did the idea for the Re35 originally come about?

'It started out as an exercise in brand design. It
was the kind of work we like doing. So instead
of waiting for a client we just did the work
for a product we really wanted to exist, and
we wanted to see how believable we could get
it. We were working on the project on and off
(whenever we had some spare time) for about
a year.'

When did you first realize that the site had seemingly gone viral?

'We started getting a lot of emails. Our service
provider called us and told us he was shutting
down the site because of what he thought was
a DoS attack. And then, of course, we checked
our analytics and found out most people were
coming to us through Twitter.'

Did you start to receive interested emails?

'Pretty soon the emails were getting out of
hand. We couldn't get through to our "regular"
messages. Most people who wrote to us
thought the product was real. A lot of people
in discussions and on Twitter were very
suspicious though…'

Planned spontaneity: Planned events being
jacked by brands and individuals across the
globe. It's all about the cultural calendar. The
following colour case studies bring these genius
campaigns to life.

3

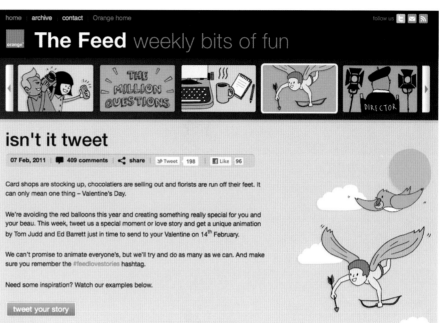

home | archive | contact | Orange home

The Feed weekly bits of fun

follow us

THE MILLION QUESTIONS

DIRECTOR

isn't it tweet

07 Feb, 2011 | 💬 409 comments | share | Tweet 198 | Like 96

Card shops are stocking up, chocolatiers are selling out and florists are run off their feet. It can only mean one thing – Valentine's Day.

We're avoiding the red balloons this year and creating something really special for you and your beau. This week, tweet us a special moment or love story and get a unique animation by Tom Judd and Ed Barrett just in time to send to your Valentine on 14th February.

We can't promise to animate everyone's, but we'll try and do as many as we can. And make sure you remember the #feedlovestories hashtag.

Need some inspiration? Watch our examples below.

tweet your story

The Feed
Valentine's Day

📢 Orange

✎ Poke London

📍 UK

🕐 February 2011

Do you believe in love at first retweet? Why avoid Twitter on Valentine's Day? Orange and their agency Poke embraced its syrupy sameness with their 'Isn't It Tweet' campaign. Followers would tweet their 140-character love stories to Orange's The Feed platform (see page 172) and animators Tom and Ed turned the best ones into ten-second animated rom-coms. The London-based duo even created sound effects. They were operating under true Urgent Genius extreme deadlines, creating a great campaign with serious longevity in no time at all. 'Isn't It Tweet' lives perfectly in the instantaneous world we enjoy. It put smiles on faces and even made us at Urgent Genius HQ gush a bit too much about it. Sorry, our secret's out. We love these guys.

We were eating chips in the rain under a tree,

Tom was a dog man.

Met at work thru a shared love of staplers.

@georgerosier: I had a big crush on Alice...

I wore a train costume,

I proposed to Olenka under an olive tree

'The crux of the job was spontaneity.'
Ed Barrett, Animator on The Feed

Shout
Your Love

📢 AT&T

✍ BBDO New York

📍 USA

🕐 2011

If a lumberjack shouted a romantic ode to you from the craggiest of peaks, would you listen? AT&T gambled on this unusual concept as people texted thousands of messages just in time for Valentine's Day. The best ones were picked and sent to the AT&T-powered phones of several 'mountain men'. In just one day, these husky characters delivered 700 'love shouts', which were filmed and posted onto recipients' Facebook walls in real time. Needless to say, this campaign echoed well beyond Valentine's Day. Just like true love should, right? And as a concept, it had echoes of Urgent Genius all over it – especially its instant approval-and-response mechanism.

A Valentine's Day campaign
with a difference.

Don't Hate on Kate

 Monorex art collective

 Stika

 UK

2011

What tools are required to defend a princess? For street artist Stika, it was spray cans. That's just what Kate needed right before the Royal Wedding after a pointless doc about her extended family fuelled a bit of 'Kate Hate'. Stika's graphically bold message was timed perfectly and its positive sentiment grabbed headlines around the world. Sometimes, Urgent Genius is all about riding against the tide, and graffiti is a great way to achieve this. Often planned and painted in minutes, it has the urgency built in. The genius is in the capable hands and cans of the artist. Oh, and the social-media and PR machine that must get behind it to go global.

'We need some kind of quick-fire art response, alongside all the craziness.'
Stika

THANKS FOR THE FREE DAY OFF.

HRH PRINCE WILLIAM & KATE MIDDLETON'S
4 DAY BENDER. 29TH APRIL - 2ND MAY 2011

Alternative Royal Wedding Plates

 KK Outlet

 KK Outlet

UK

2011

A topical in-joke that went viral almost by accident, these plates tapped into the mix of scepticism and celebration surrounding the Royal Wedding. Created within forty-eight hours of the wedding announcement, the plates were a timely response to the news that there was a two-week wait for the official plates. KK Outlet's 'commemorative china' wasn't originally meant for sale, but the online buzz was so loud they decided to produce them.

A Royal Wedding plate for the Facebook generation.

T-Mobile Royal Wedding

 T-Mobile

 Saatchi & Saatchi

 UK

 2011

Louis Spence, East 17 and *Four Weddings and a Funeral* all have one thing in common: T-Mobile. When Kate and Wills announced they were to be married, Saatchi & Saatchi didn't hang around. Taking inspiration from YouTube's infamous 'JK Wedding Entrance Dance', they created the 'Royal Wedding Dance', selecting over 130 extras from a Facebook casting call to produce a spoof video that appeared to show a hilarious all-singing, all-dancing start to the royal wedding. Filmed in St Bartholomew's Church, which also featured in the aforementioned rom-com, to East 17's banging 'House of Love', this Louis Spence-choreographed spectacle pulled in a whopping 26 million views and endless amounts of press coverage, all before it aired on television.

A right royal knees up.

World Cup Octopuppy

 Burger King

 Publicis

 Singapore

 2010

As Paul the Octopus was hijacking the global headlines by predicting German World Cup results through his feeding habits, Publicis Singapore was stretching a tiny budget by opting for a Facebook-powered lottery. They put Rebel the Octopuppy in charge of choosing the snack customers wanted. Simple promotion: If you guessed the pup's pick, you won that item. While not rocket science, we'd bet a truckload of octopus burgers that a certain eight-appendaged mollusc helped maximize PR for this campaign.

'The entire process had to be thought through the moment we came up with the idea.'

Valerie Cheng

Play BK Quick Pick or I will tickle you till you squeal like a little girl.

Dutch Celebration Shirt

 Self-promotion

 Wonder Years

Netherlands

 2010

Imagine a stadium full of half-naked fans celebrating Holland winning the World Cup? Creatives Bas and Daan at Wonder Years almost made this happen. By printing the faces of Holland's stars on the insides of bright-orange shirts, they transformed the simple tee into a famous goal celebration. This is further evidence that Urgent Genius doesn't have to come from ad agencies or big brands with cash. It's about spotting an opportunity for some tactical fun and executing it quickly on a tight budget.

'Some well-known blogs started writing about it. From there it took flight.'
Bas van de Poel and Daan van Dam

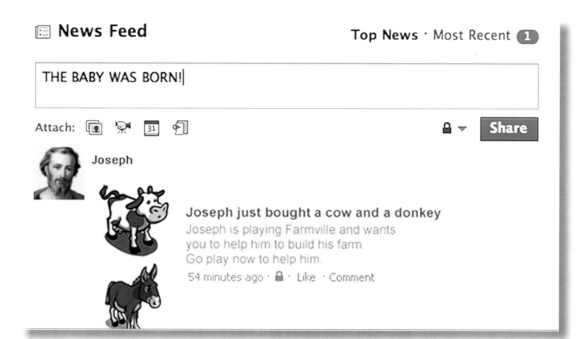

The Digital Nativity

📢 Self-promotion

✍ Excentric

📍 Portugal

🕐 2010

Your girlfriend texts you: 'In labour with miracle God baby. Get the donkey.' Would you panic or sort something out online? Lisbon-based agency Excentric faced questions like this as they retold the story of the Nativity using social platforms such as Twitter and Facebook, as well as sites like Wikipedia, Amazon and Google Maps. Mixing two subjects people are passionate about – religion and the internet – Excentric created what Advertising Age claimed was the biggest viral debut since Old Spice's 'Response' campaign (see page 182).

The following of a Twitter-based star, and a crash course in how to buy a donkey on Farmville

The Super Social Christmas Tree

 Heineken

 iris worldwide Singapore

 Singapore

 December 2011

Wouldn't holidays be less hectic if you were a Christmas bauble? With Heineken's Super Social Christmas Tree, you could just dangle there atop an 11-m-high (36 ft) tree decorated with forty-eight huge LCD screens. Designed by iris Singapore, this digital evergreen was populated by a Facebook app that let users submit photo ornaments and messages to be displayed on the screens. Heineken then sent their followers videos of themselves on the tree for them to share: a bit of real-time personalization to top off this perfect festive cocktail of digital-meets-real-world. Wait, what about carols? This tree needed some Heineken-fuelled carollers, surely – so a virtual choir of singers from around the world made sure the night was far from silent.

A forty-eight-LCD-screened tree connected to Facebook

Surprise Christmas Presents

 Spanair

 Shackleton

 Spain

 December 2010

People want to be home on Christmas Day, not in an airport. Spanair decided to capitalize on this in a beautiful way. Their last flight on Christmas Eve from Barcelona to Las Palmas arrived a few minutes past midnight, so it was perfect timing to provide personalized Christmas presents for passengers at the luggage reclaim. Passengers were surprised to find personally addressed presents each containing a gift based on the information they'd provided the airline (age, sex, etc). The arrivals hall burst into applause. News networks and blogs always look for a heartwarming story at Christmas and this stunt proved perfect, living on in a touching YouTube short film about the experiment, attracting over 700,000 views in the two weeks after Christmas.

An unexpected publicity coup.

The Shamrock Shake

 McDonalds

 Leo Burnett Chicago

 USA

 March 2009

If you spot two leprechauns turning a river Irish green with a one-ton milkshake, you're either double lucky or drunk, right? No. You're McDonald's and Leo Burnett, and your Shamrock Shake stunt's just piggybacked Chicago's annual St Patrick's Day dyeing of the river. Thanks to their visual trick, it looked like the work of a couple of clumsy leprechauns with an oversized milkshake. It was actually a motorboat with an 8-foot-long (2.4 m) Plexiglas Shamrock Shake cup with a green foam trail. It got buzz online, in newspapers and even on television. To us, this wasn't lucky. It was genius. And planned to look spontaneous. Even better.

The river gets dyed green every year – it was just waiting to happen.

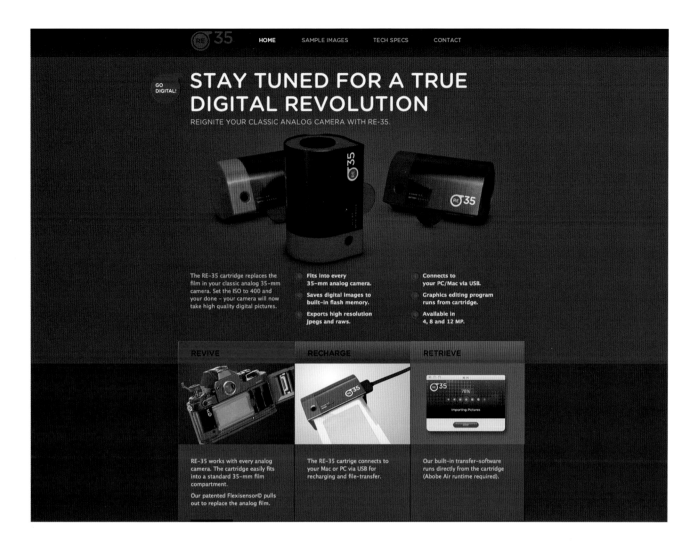

The RE-35 cartridge replaces the film in your classic analog 35-mm camera. Set the ISO to 400 and your done – your camera will now take high quality digital pictures.

- Fits into every 35-mm analog camera.
- Saves digital images to built-in flash memory.
- Exports high resolution jpegs and raws.

- Connects to your PC/Mac via USB.
- Graphics editing program runs from cartridge.
- Available in 4, 8 and 12 MP.

REVIVE

RE-35 works with every analog camera. The cartridge easily fits into a standard 35-mm film compartment.

Our patented Flexisensor© pulls out to replace the analog film.

RECHARGE

The RE-35 cartrige connects to your Mac or PC via USB for recharging and file-transfer.

RETRIEVE

Our built-in transfer-software runs directly from the cartridge (Abobe Air runtime required).

The Re35

📢 Self-promotion

✍ Rogge & Pott

📍 Germany

🕐 2011

Create something that everyone would want but didn't know existed – that's a great Urgent Genius brief. And that's exactly what Hamburg-based design firm Rogge & Pott did when they designed a USB device that resembles an old 35 mm roll and transforms analogue film cameras into digital ones. They launched the site on 1 April and some saw through it, noticing certain drawbacks (i.e. no digital display screen), but the fact that a disclaimer had to be put on the website proved its success. And then the comments online proved that there was a real desire for it. In fact, the pranksters themselves claim to be looking into making it for real. Or is this another joke? Not sure. What we do know is that April Fool's Day is a perfect training ground to mess with people's minds, especially if you can tap into the techie zeitgeist.

I'M BACK!

It started out as an exercise in brand design....Pretty soon the emails were getting out of hand.

Henning, Rogge & Pott

Home Products Apparel
Events Company Info

**THRILLER ENERGY
MAXIMUM CONSCIOUSNESS™**

Thriller Energy - a specially designed new energy formula to thrill
your mind. Achieve Maximum Consciousness™ for your
maximum lifestyle with Thriller Energy. Packed with b vitamins,
taurine, gingko and loads of other stuff that will have you
slamming your old life into the trash. No slow all go with Thriller
Energy. Enhanced Life™ with Thriller Energy!

© 2009 Thriller Energy Inc.

Thriller Drinks

 Self-promotion

 Fucked Up

 USA

 2010

A punk band called Fucked Up. Legions of fans who love them because they're
slightly, no, totally unhinged. Add a sense of humour and April Fool's Day
and you've got instant PR headlines. The band announced on their blog that
they were being sued by one of their supposed 2010 SXSW sponsors, energy-
drink brand Thriller, following a recent tirade of theirs against the brand. The
band had even gone to the trouble of designing a convincing website for the
non-existent drink. This brilliantly executed April Fool was so convincing
it triggered a web petition on their behalf within a day. As fans were venting
their anger at Thriller, the band's online support soared and then sank
immediately when a Canadian music channel reminded fans it was 1 April.

> 'There were countless
> internet stories, we did radio
> interviews...it really took off
> in just a few hours.'
> Mike Haliechuk, Fucked Up

Virgin Volcanic

 Virgin

 Virgin

 International

 April 2012

'Screw business as usual.' Literally. Richard Branson's not happy with conquering space when he can build a giant screw to dig into the centre of the earth to show people what it's like to live a life of lava love. A press release announced Virgin Travel's intentions to send travellers deep into the ground as part of a new initiative called 'Virgin Volcanic'. Before the public could book tickets, however, it was revealed to be a hoax. Other than being a unique April Fool, the Urgent Genius of this is that it further solidified Virgin's space exploration venture by highlighting their pioneering spirit, albeit in an absurd manner. The stunt was less timely than purely bizarre, but the subsequent tweets from celebrities including Seth Green and Tom Hanks announcing their places on the first voyage were inspired. For us, this stunt shows us how maverick Mr Branson is. And how perfect his brand would be for our next Urgent Genius Weekender (see page 186).

> 'I have long held a fascination with volcanoes....What can I say, I lava challenge.'
> Richard Branson

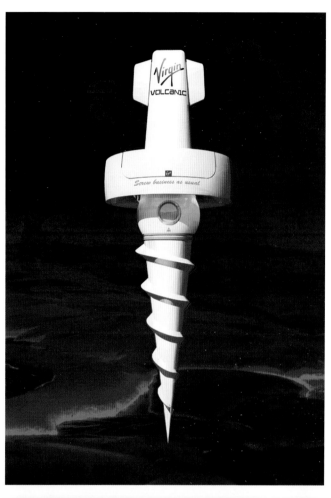

FRESH HOT

'We worked with one of the world's leading micro-biologists.'

Anthony Ganjou, Curb Media

4. Keep it fresh

This is the toughest chapter to write, because what feels very unique and different now may be just the start of a revolution that's in full swing by the time you read this. That doesn't mean it's time to skip this chapter altogether. Sure, we'd rather see the words and case studies magically update in real time like the billboards do in *Minority Report*, and yes, we're working on that. But for now, view this snapshot of some of the most innovative case studies we were covering on UrgentGenius.com before the book went to print. And be sure to use the QR codes dotted around these pages to go straight to the good stuff on our website.

For us, it's the mindset employed by the creative heroes in this chapter that we want to highlight. I'm sure the Brazilian creative team that printed customers' faces on burger wrappers almost instantly have gone on to innovate with robotics or 3D printing, or something that's not been invented yet. And what about the guys you'll read about who raised their name-and-shame game to new levels by pointing out those who are rubbish at parking and putting their crimes on ad banners in real time. We know there's something special going on with these folks.

So what's the common thread? Well, it's what we call the Urgent Genius mindset. It's their approach to solving a problem creatively. We think the creators you'll meet here are maverick in their single-minded approach to disrupting the status quo. The best clients are more digitally savvy and are constantly asking for the next big thing. But one basic question is answered in every brief:
What's never been done before – and, where appropriate, what new tool can I use in a surprising way?

Something crucial to fast-iterating content is the ability to determine quickly the feasibility of a project you wish to embark on. To this end, when you're in the digital space, it's hugely beneficial to have a technical mind. This isn't to say that a degree in computing is required to make something brilliant – not at all – but understanding the limitations, or cool new features, in the 'next big technology' may just give you the edge against the competition.

Take the Arduino, for example. It simmered below the horizon for quite some time, then exploded in popularity, to the point that you can now pick up a starter kit on most high streets. For quick prototyping and proving concepts, the Arduino offers a cheap platform to get your idea out there quickly.

But do you buy your whole tech team an Arduino, and have them play around with making an LED blink for a day? It's easily argued that there would be good value in it, as you now have a room full of people who understand the capabilities and limitations of a new device. With the Raspberry Pi booming in popularity, our horizons seem limitless – we can now drop fully operational, connected computers into boxes the size of a cigarette case. To pass this real-world opportunity up could be foolish; however, you've always got to consider how your real-world object connects back to a relatable campaign that people worldwide can appreciate. There is limited value in delighting ten people in Soho, London, if their experience with your installation doesn't translate well to film. Think about microsites, and think about partner campaigns. Get the people local to the installation/device excited and curious, but don't leave people who can't interact with it feeling they're missing out to the point of disappointment.

How have we embraced all of this? Like curious children. We've brought in top specialists to teach us, like the guy who's leading the Arduino hackers/makers movement in the UK. He was great. Our tech team in London getting a day off to geek out with electronics? We've already seen massive benefits. Especially if you follow up with a hack day that produces such acts of Urgent Genius as Paul Curry's 'SwearCopter' – a helicopter that only flies when you drop a steady stream of C- and F-bombs. Oh and don't forget London College of Communication's Fred The Shred. This is a cross between a Tamagotchi and a paper shredder. Fred 'reads' what's being shred and reacts with an appropriate sound. So a catcall for a picture of Jennifer Aniston and a yawn for a legal document. You get the drill.

'If an agency doesn't have an R&D department, it might as well have a noose around its neck waiting for the client to kick the chair from under them.'

Sam Ball, Lean Mean Fighting Machine

Here's a question for you: How do you keep connected to the best minds in the industry? You bring speakers in every week for a 'Working Lunch'. Agency Republic, one of the first proper digital agencies that Jon worked for, did this and it was insanely popular. We're building a LinkedIn list of interesting folks to bring in to inspire those we're working with. Check them out at LinkedInteresting.com.

We'd like to know what you're doing to keep people fresh – let us know at urgentgenius.com.

In this chapter we'll examine examples where the creators have thought long and hard about creating something truly innovative. Some have achieved that through technical innovation, while others have flipped the issue on its head and approached it from a totally new perspective. From working with microbiologists to develop the right type of material, to physical structures virtually enabled, we'll explore what it takes to keep your thinking fresh.

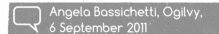

Carl Jones, Grey Canada, 8 February 2011

Frustrated at the lack of interest in their experimental idea, ad agency Grey Canada decided to launch this piece of Urgent Genius as an advert for themselves. The Global Mood Clock (see page 98) brings traditional office wall clocks into a new era, with an app that scans Twitter, Google and Flickr and aggregates the results to calculate the prevailing mood of a city. New York, Los Angeles, Moscow, Rio, Tokyo and Shanghai all have their own Mood Clocks thanks to geo-tagged social media.

Firstly, how did the idea for the clocks come about?

'I travel a lot, and when I would go to check the time for various world cities I felt there was an opportunity there to show more than just time. I wanted to see more of what was happening in each of those cities; what was the mood in that city, how did it feel? So in early 2010 when I moved to Grey Canada, I explained the seed of my idea to a few people. One of the art directors Todd Lawson understood my concept and was able to interpret the idea into a physical design. Then Toby Pilling came onto the project and wrote a program to read Flickr images and select the dominant colour of the latest ten pictures. From that we were able to represent the mood of the city by referring the dominant colour to a chromatherapy chart that we had created.'

How did you go about partnering with Google, Twitter and Flickr to create the clock?

'We didn't ask Google, Twitter or foursquare for permission; we basically designed an aggregator app that took the information available for free. Their software is open source so all we had to do is ask for their API key and they let us know their ground rules. From Flickr, we used their API to create software that would look at the geo-located images to read the dominant colour. From Google and Twitter we pulled in geo-located top trending words. We used pieces of each, though I can't say any one source was used more than another.'

Was it also a comment on the weird melting pot of international news we're fed every day?

'Yes – with this digital explosion there is so much data coming at you all the time. I think our job as advertisers is to simplify information in a way that is meaningful. The clock is a product of what's out there though, and can be a bit funny or bizarre too – I remember when the top trending Twitter word in London, UK, was #greatgrannygangbang. I was thinking: "Huh? What is that?"'

Angela Bassichetti, Ogilvy, 6 September 2011

The following example was both funny and slightly invasive. It grabbed people's attention in a surprising way. In a bid to remind Whopper fans that you can 'Have it Your Way', Burger King and Ogilvy Brazil gave the 'custom order' new meaning with Whopper Face (see page 99). A hidden camera snapped customers as they ordered their food, and then surprised them when the burger arrived in a wrapper adorned with a picture of their face. A customer gallery featured on Burger King's main website, while a video of the campaign climbed to 111,000 views on YouTube.

How did the idea come about and what were the challenges?

'Ogilvy Brazil had just won the BK pitch and during the first briefing the creatives came up with the idea. The client loved the idea, but there was no budget for extras actions, and this was the first problem we faced. If we were to do it, we would need to implement the idea with a low budget. And we had other obstacles: taking the photo without the customer noticing it, and without disturbing the workflow at the store. And the biggest of them all: pulling off the whole process without making the customer wait more than they usually do for their Whopper. This idea took almost a year to be implemented.'

Whopper Face is all over the blogosphere and online media, but did it get much coverage in Brazil itself?

'Whopper Face was created for online media. We didn't use any resources to promote this promo

beyond the digital. We didn't even spend money to promote the video on YouTube. We just posted it and everything happened by itself.'

Customers are getting used to expecting personalization. Do you think advertising has shifted in this direction permanently, or is it just a phase?

'I don't think personalization is a purpose in itself. I think it's just an artifice to grab the consumer's attention. I believe technology is the enabler to narrow the relationship between brand and consumer.'

 Simon Higby, DDB Stockholm, July 2011

To promote a ski edition of the Passat, equipped to deal with frozen terrain and low temperatures, agency DDB Stockholm left their campaign at the mercy of the elements (see page 100). A billboard poster of the car was positioned on a frozen lake, advertising a special offer which was 'Winter Adjusted' to match the car, and which would expire as soon as the ice melted. The campaign's website invited visitors to bet on the date it would go under, with the prize of a VIP racing day at Gothenburg for the closest guess.

What prompted the idea?

'We spoke to Volkswagen for a long time about combining their tactical sales communication

with product brand building. This seemed like a perfect time to do so. The Swedish winter is notoriously harsh, the Passat can take on the winter…so we thought: Why shouldn't the campaign harness it too? Volkswagen was totally supportive of the campaign and idea. We even had a deer staring directly into the webcam wondering what it was. That was quite fun.'

When did the sign first start to gain attention?

'The sign generated a response almost right away. This was helped by an above-the-line media spend – traditional media is at its best in some ways when supporting an online element in a campaign. Especially on the Swedish market, which has a high online cut through.'

Did you worry about people tampering with the sign to make it melt faster?

'Yes we did think about that, so we kept the location a secret, which worked. However, it would have been fun and maybe added to the talk value should someone have tampered with the sign.'

Charlotte Bates, Connected Pictures, October 2011

The digital agency BEING created a real-time interactive experience bringing Caribbean sunshine to cloudy Britain to show passers-by what they were missing (see page 107). They created the first live digital billboard event across continents. Presenters were streamed live from a secret Caribbean location (St Lucia) as they interacted with the public on a rainy Saturday in London. The billboard was live for two full days, but for the week running up to the live billboard, 'teaser' films were shown to generate interest.

Were there any challenges or glitches with this brilliant campaign?

'One challenge was to hold the audience's attention using outdoor media. The digital billboard answered this challenge by making outdoor media as real-time, interactive and social as other media. There were also technical challenges involved with creating a live feed from the Caribbean location, and internet ports had to be specially rewired to the beach to enable the production team to achieve a full-quality stream.'

Describe the social element of the campaign.

'The audience was invited to ask questions via text and Facebook, and ultimately to guess the location for the chance to win a holiday there.

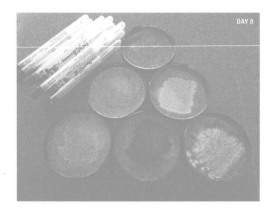

DAY 0

While the billboard was live, more than one text per minute was received. The average time passers-by spent watching was forty-five seconds, compared to an industry average of just one or two seconds.'

Anthony Ganjou, Curb Media, 1 June 2012

In Canada, the world's first bacterial billboard announced the release of the new Steven Soderbergh film *Contagion* (see page 104). On 28 August, Lowe Roche Toronto created it with the help of CURB media and a couple of microbiologists. Two giant Petri dishes were painted with live bacteria and they multiplied over seven days to spell out the name of the film. As a living billboard that played out in real time, we think it was truly Urgent Genius.

How did the idea come about?

'Lowe Roche contacted CURB with the view to creating a billboard out of bacteria, fully in the mindset that it was an impossible task. Within forty-eight hours not only had we shown how it was possible but we were able to offer them a choice of colours and also time parameters for the message to develop. We also opened the opportunity of having different types of words and logos rather than just a shape.'

Can you elaborate on the type of bacteria used?

'The thirty-five or so microbes used in the *Contagion* billboards were obtained from suppliers in Canada – we thought better of carrying luggage filled with bacterial and fungal containers on a flight to North America. The billboard's striking blood-like colour comes from the red-pigmented bacterium *Serratia marcescens.* Some of the visual impact was due to chance: bacteria and mould from the outside air also took hold in each billboard before they were sealed.'

How quickly did the bacteria multiply to expose the message?

'The bacteria cultivated over seven days as had been planned since the beginning.'

How much media exposure did it create?

'$5 million national and international PR offline and 500,000 YouTube views. It was the most successful movie launch in Canada during 2011. Using an inspiring medium can generate enormous (and quite literally viral) impact on and offline. Within a week the idea had been featured on blogs, news channels and media on every single continent on the planet.'

The Village newspaper in Russia launched an app in 2012 tackling the Russian epidemic of bad parking (see page 111). Crowd-sourced images of offenders, uploaded via the app, utilized number-plate recognition. This then added the offending cars into ad units that obstructed the copy on the pages they were placed on. They cleverly used IP detection so the cars you see are offenders in your area. This real-time use of technology then encouraged the viewer to remove the offender by clicking 'share', hence spreading the word of the offending car to more people. It was a name-and-shame campaign in real time using smart technology.

Where did the idea come from?

'*The Village* is an online city newspaper that really cares for the city…it supports many social initiatives. The problem of illegal parking has become a huge problem in Moscow and other big cities in Russia. We decided to help solve it with an idea that named and shamed those impolite people. We decided that a mobile application could be an easy tool for people to become "agents" of "Parking Douche hunt". We then integrated the application and the display ad into one smart and IP-targeted campaign.'

How long did it take to develop?

'About a month. We started to work on the project in March and launched it in April. We put a lot of thinking into location targeting for display ads using browser location and also the API of popular Russian map service Yandex.Maps. We actually changed the display ad several times before the launch to make it noticeable and a little bit annoying on the page, but not too annoying.'

How successful was the campaign?

'For us it's a long-term project – we plan to have it live for at least one to two years. But we're happy to say that the first period of its launch was very successful. We've recruited many app users, and generated many views and shares. The idea has gained a lot of international support: we've received a lot of letters and offers from people in the United States, UK, Germany and other countries who want to develop the project there. Now we are working on an app that supports several languages and hope that "Parking Douche" will soon enough become an international platform to cope with impolite and illegal parking.'

Keeping it fresh: getting the unique angle and moving on it FAST. Check out a few of the key elements of the campaigns we've looked at in the following colour pages.

The Life
Scoreboard

📢 PUMA

✍ Droga5

📍 International

🕐 2009

Who'd win a cage match: Jonas Brothers or Insane Clown Posse? Don't answer that. Let Puma's Life Scoreboard do it. It enables you to make a competition out of anything by putting it to the vote among users. By creating their own social network, PUMA not only tapped into the competitive nature of their customers but also found a way to get real-time results that show ever-changing opinion on topical issues such as the 2012 U.S. Presidential election, one of the most popular scoreboards. Of course, this is why we love it. For us, it's a newsjacking tool to gauge sentiment in a fun way. And a successful one at that. The campaign gained mind share and web share 20 per cent higher than PUMA's normal base level.

Life's more fun when you keep score.

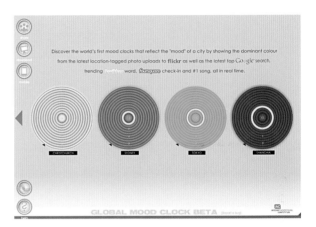

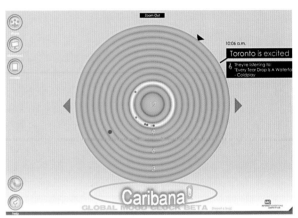

Global Mood Clock

 Self-promotion

 Grey Canada

Canada

 January 2011

Cities have feelings, too, y'know! Or so Grey Canada believe. Inspired to update the classic 'wall of clocks' that adorn most international offices, they created the 'Global Mood Clock'. This app takes data from social-media platforms to show exactly how each major city is feeling, all in real time. To work all this out, it was programmed to display trending tweets, topics and hashtags and also to find the most common colour in each city's Flickr uploads. On top of all that multi-tasking, it even behaves as a clock should, giving you the time of day.

'There is so much data coming at you all the time...our job is to simplify information in a way that is meaningful.'

Carl Jones, Grey Canada

Whopper Face

 Burger King

 Ogilvy

 Brazil

March 2010

Jesus popping up on your morning toast is pretty cool, but Ogilvy did one better. They took a surreptitious picture of each Whopper customer, printed it on the wrapper, served it up to them and filmed their delight. Within hours, Whopper Face customers lit up the internet with photos, videos and blog posts, creating mass-demand for this project in franchises. In the time it took to flame-grill a patty, they made the customer feel like a King.

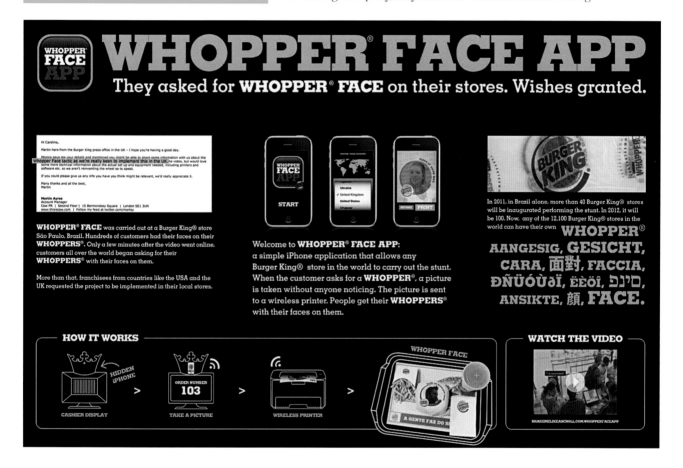

'Technology is the enabler to narrow the relationship between brand and consumer...'

Angela Bassichetti, Ogilvy

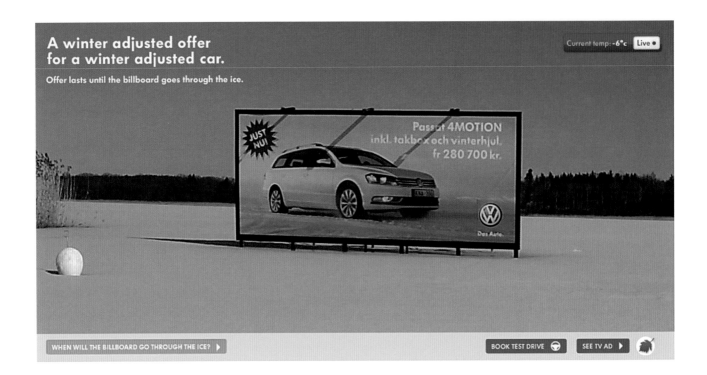

Winter
Adjusted Offer

 VW Sweden

 DDB Stockholm

 Sweden

March 2011

The next offer isn't available while supplies last. In fact, it ripped the rule book for limited-time offer ads to shreds. With a bit of clever Urgent Genius thinking, DDB and VW reinvented the hurry-and-spend retail tactic by telling customers to take their sweet slow time. Taking full advantage of the harsh Swedish winter, they told customers that the offer ended when the ad broke the ice. They were encouraged to guess when that would happen to win a day at the races. The billboard was streamed live twenty-four hours a day, and on 14 April 2011 the sign finally sank. 3,002 cars were sold in just two months – a 38 per cent increase over the previous year. By having a sense of Urgent Genius, a humble billboard was turned into an online sensation.

Almost immediately the sign generated a response.

Melting
QR Codes

 WWF

 iris worldwide Amsterdam

📍 Netherlands

 February 2012

The Brief: save the world, by advertising on melting ice. Budget: ZERO. Deadline: twenty-four hours. That's a real toughy, huh? Not for iris worldwide, who nailed it with their WWF QR codes, which directed people to WWF's site. By spotting an opportunity for some Urgent Genius 'doing' and calling in Green Graffiti, an eco-friendly media company, they used 'Sticky Sand' (sand mixed with fluid that doesn't melt ice) to embed the codes onto Amsterdam's frozen canals, without breaking ice. The 'ads' were placed in prime spots around the city, where they'd be viewed by people on their way to work. By lunchtime, images of the melting QR codes went viral, spreading on Twitter, Facebook and Pinterest. This idea took courage, which thankfully the Dutch have in pints.

'QR codes have always annoyed me. But these were melting, which made them relevant.'

Tom Ormes, iris Amsterdam

Heineken
Star Player

🔊 Heineken

✒ AKQA

📍 UK

🕐 2010

This Champions' League-based app works like
in-play betting: it turns the game into a game,
giving a high level of interaction in real time.
Players can guess when a goal will be scored,
answer trivia questions and see how they're
ranking against friends, with the latter being
shared over Twitter and Facebook. By leveraging
all 125 Champions League Games, they've
taken Urgent Genius thinking to another
level – with an audience of over 1 billion
playing for a potential 11,250 minutes, Heineken
have created a Godzilla-like monster of brand
engagement. They think it's all over...it is now.

Players could predict what happened
in the next thirty seconds.

Last.fm Festival

📢 Last.fm

✎ Rehab Studios

📍 UK

🕐 January 2010

Last.fm created the world's first user-generated music festival, hosting shows in London and New York on the same night. Then they made a set list of the most relevant bands by taking data from their 'Scrobbling' log (that tells them what people are listening to). The gigs were recorded and streamed on Last.fm and it was a great success, cementing their global brand campaign in people's minds and on their social networks. Basically, Last.fm turned it all the way up to 11, like every Urgent Genius should.

**POWERED BY
YOUR SCROBBLES**

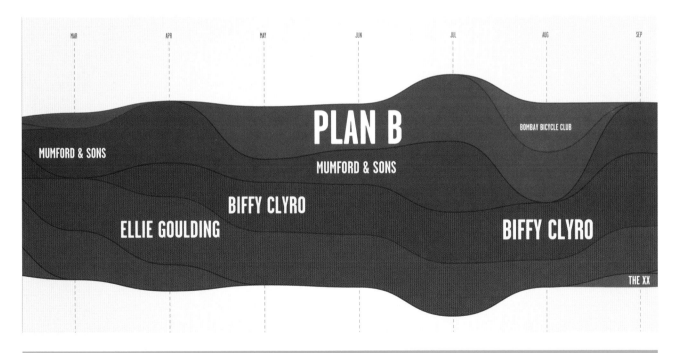

Musical tastes and trends influenced the line up and visuals at the festival.

Bacterial Billboard

 Contagion

 Lowe Roche Toronto and CURB

 Canada

 September 2011

Nothing's more urgent than a deadly virus, as Lowe Roche and CURB demonstrated with two large Petri dishes, used to promote the film *Contagion*. Harmless bacteria were used to spell the film's name on two handmade billboards. In the seven days it took the mould to grow, news of these unique ads spread, generating over 100,000 Twitter and Facebook mentions, and 405,000 YouTube views, totalling more than $3 million of earned media, with coverage in over 100 countries. We think the living billboard was truly an act of Urgent Genius. Now pass the hand sanitizer.

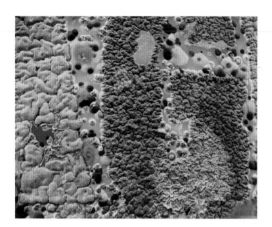

A bacterial billboard made out of thirty-five different types of microbes.

Powerade
Copa de America

 Coca-Cola

Wunderman

Argentina

July 2011

A good ol' punch up used to settle football arguments. Now Twitter does. Powerade realized this as they launched a Copa de America campaign on the platform in 2011. Their microsite used real-time graphics to visualize the fans' tweets. For a month, the platform became the go-to place in Latin America to double-check vital information such as how many people thought it should've been a red card. It worked wonders, as, in the 2,340 minutes spent online during the tournament, Powerade's fans sent a total of 455,000 tweets, boosting the brand's mind share dramatically.

Real-time infographics
on the fly.

Caribbean Live

 British Airways

 BEING and Connected Pictures

 UK

 March 2011

BA employed a bit of real-time Urgent Genius to tell shoppers in wintry London that they fly to more Caribbean islands than any other UK airline. They flew two lucky holidaymakers to a secret Caribbean island and streamed them onto a digital billboard. Passers-by could win a place next to them by guessing their location correctly. Viewers spent, on average, fifteen minutes interacting with the couple, who even managed to inspire an impromptu dance-off with the crowd.

Caribbean sunshine beamed direct to cloudy Britain.

Alan Sugar
Twitter

 Pan Macmillian

 Guided Collective

 UK

 September 2011

The original brief for the promotion of Lord Sugar's book, *The Way I See It*, asked for traditional ads, but a tiny budget demanded something else. So Guided Collective put on their Urgent Genius hats to create the world's first Twitter book signing. The day before the event, they encouraged his fans, over social media, to send in questions. The best ones got a copy of his book and a live-streamed message of him signing it, which was shareable over Facebook. The results were incredible: #TheWayISeeIt trended globally for twenty hours, they got 100,000 views in thirty minutes and 8,000 new followers for Alan himself.

390,000 tweets and the No. 1 globally trending topic on Twitter.

Tim Horton Coffee News

 Tim Horton and Gulf News

 Y&R Dubai

 UAE

June 2012

Physical morning ritual: coffee. Digital morning ritual: getting your news via Twitter. Dubai's largest English-language newspaper *Gulf News* and Y&R Dubai asked the popular coffee chain Tim Hortons to print the *Gulf News* Twitter feed in real time on their cups. Result: nearly 3,000 new followers in the first fortnight. Traffic rose by 41 per cent and subscriptions more than doubled. We feel that taking digital things into the real world is the future of Urgent Genius, so thank you Mr Horton for your clever cups.

The coffee cup became the morning paper.

Toyota
Backseat Driver

Toyota

Party

Japan

2011

Ever wanted your car to poop out prizes? Thought you'd never hear the phrase 'poop out prizes' in a sentence? Well, the car-maker's toy brand ToyToyota and Tokyo agency Party created Cannes Gold-winning Backseat Driver, which does just that. They created a game so kids can drive down the same road their parents are driving on at the same time. The Urgent Genius of this is its real-time interactivity. The iPhone's GPS informs the game so it can animate the real world. You just steer your virtual car around behind 'Papa Car' (the car you're physically travelling in), collecting prize 'emissions' released by Papa Car so you can buy upgrades and add-ons. Once the journey is over, share it on Twitter for all to see that you, a grown adult, have been playing it for hours and haven't shared it with your toddler yet.

Backseat Driver puts the kids in the driving seat.

BOLSHAYA LUBIANKA STREET MOSCOW

o250кв 197

Parking Douche

 The Village

 Look at Me

Russia

May 2012

The Village, Moscow's popular online newspaper, created this wonderful app to name and shame bad parkers in pure Urgent Genius splendour. Users upload photos of offending vehicles, which are then converted into live, geo-located banner ads, so that they only appear in the local area, meaning viewers can actually see the car in question. Geo-tagged awesomeness is definitely the way forward, and the real-time element here blows our minds. It's no surprise that the perfectly named Parking Douche has been a huge success, with a traffic response of over 70 per cent – so much so that it's now in demand across the world and even featured on television programme *Top Gear*. Who needs traffic wardens when you have web-savvy vigilantes?

Name and shame in real time.

'There is to be no joining of the mo to the sideburns (that's considered a beard).'

The rules of Movember

5. Invent your own event

Topical relevance is hard to come by, so why not fix the chances in your favour? The case studies in this chapter show brands using their influence to create fun, novelty days of the year, with the chance to revive them annually.

For the last few years, we have been watching Wonderbra take ownership of cleavage globally with the creation of International Cleavage Day (see page 122), which started before social media existed but came into its own when sharing photos online took off.

The formula was simple: take one iconic brand, a nation of women and a subject guaranteed to turn heads. Let your campaign loose on social media, and let the eye candy do the rest. Founded in South Africa in 2002, this 'invented holiday' recurs every April, inviting women to share cleavage photos online and celebrate girl power, while Wonderbra donate revenue from their sales to the cancer charity The Sunflower Fund.

Do you celebrate your cleavage once a year? What about National Day of Unplugging (see page 126) or any of the ones we've included on the Urgent Genius Cultural Calender on page 134? These invented events pop up on the calendar faster than you can down a Krispy Kreme on National Donut Day. Who makes up these days and are they effective? Some of these events are created by brands. Others are created by passionate individuals. Inventing a movement is no easy task.

Firstly, you need to make sure your movements are created for the right reasons. Scott Goodson in his brilliant book on cultural movements states:

'Movements – at least, the kind of movements that gather around positive, creative, dynamic ideas – can help build a better, fairer, more sustainable, and more interesting world. They can help individuals to rally support for worthy causes; help an innovator build momentum behind a new idea; they can even put someone in the White House. From a business standpoint, they can enable a company to form a stronger connection to the public. And yes, that certainly can translate into profit, though I think it can also have other effects that are less mercenary but no less important.'

Another thing we look for in these movements is to make sure they're not overbranded and that they reflect what people are thinking and talking about online. Next you need to make sure that your movement has something that people can believe in or be passionate about. To quote Goodson again: 'If a public groundswell occurs without altering people's attitudes or shifting the cultural dialogue at least slightly, then it's not a movement – it's just a fad.'

So how do you create an event that becomes an important part of the cultural conversation? If your created event's a hit, the day becomes self-perpetuating. Then, brands can riff on their own fame as their creation takes on the level of a small-scale movement.

In this chapter, we want to explore a few questions. How do you know if your movement will achieve a level of authenticity required for it to scale? What narrative approaches are best for communicating your story? What technology and tools are needed to make sure people hear about you? What triggers in culture are best to ride to make sure your movement falls on receptive ears? What are the signs that your movement's been a success and how do you evaluate it afterwards?

 Adam Garone, Movember, 27 July 2012

In 2003, men's health issues got their own international day (see page 132). And men all around the world now had a worthy excuse to release their inner Tom Selleck. A rare branded calendar event-turned household name, Movember spans an entire month and

'[Invented events] are only successful because of ongoing marketing campaigns that re-invent the occasion. Most spring from grass-roots initiatives, many involving challenges.'

Susan F. Benjamin *Flash*

portmanteaus 'Moustache' and 'November'. Mo Bros are challenged to grow a moustache for the thirty days and thirty nights of November. The movement has bred a sub-culture of ironic, moustachioed hipsters, and Movember has raised over $300 million USD worldwide. There are rules: 'There is to be no joining of the mo to the sideburns (that's considered a beard); there's to be no joining of the handlebars to the chin (that's considered a goatee); and each Mo Bro must conduct himself like a true gentleman.'

Where did the idea originate? Who was involved? What were the inspirations behind this truly original movement?

'Movember was born in 2003 in a bar in Melbourne, Australia: a group of thirty mates decided to have some fun by bringing back the old-school moustache like the ones worn by their fathers and sporting heroes.'

What do you consider to be the tipping point of the Movember movement?

'The tipping point for Movember was early on in 2005, when we realized that what was originally a bit of fun between friends had the potential to inspire and engage a wide audience, raising awareness and funds that could change the face of men's health.'

Digital has been at the heart of Movember. What has been most successful creative execution of the campaign?

'The most significant and successful creative digital development has been the introduction of the 'Mo Space' feature on the Movember website in 2007. This allows participants to record their unique Movember journey and more easily share it with their networks to raise awareness and provide a fundraising platform. In more recent years, Mo Space has also included integration

RAGE AGAINST TERRIBLE POP MUSIC: HOW TO START A MOVEMENT AGAINST SIMON COWELL

What about an Urgent Genius movement designed to react against popular culture and subvert trends? With social media, it's possible to create movements that react against trending topics in a subversive way by mobilizing the bitter riot mob.

For our money, there's no better use of Urgent Genius thinking than getting hipsters and rebels (and normal folk like us) to rid the world of saccharine, über-bland music. That's why we salute one of the best examples of newsjacking in aid of creating a cultural movement.

When we start giving out Urgent Genius awards, we will surely honour the legends that are Jon and Tracy Morter, the London-based duo who successfully prevented Simon Cowell's *X-Factor* winners from being number one in the charts at Christmas, which in Britain is quite an honour.

Jon and Tracy launched a hugely successful campaign to keep *The X-Factor*'s Joe McElderry from becoming number one with his cover, proposing Rage Against the Machine's 'Killing in the Name' instead and launching a Facebook account named 'Rage Against the Machine for Christmas No 1'. The grass-roots movement worked. It kept McElderry away from the top spot on Christmas week, breaking the domination of *X-Factor* hits at Christmas. The successful campaign also raised over £163,000 for homeless charity Shelter.

with social-media channels and automatically generated emails.'

How would you describe your campaign's sense of urgency – responding in real-time with an idea that captures the zeitgeist of online conversations?

'Movember prides itself on having a real-time and grass-roots connection with its audience. This is applied both online and offline. With only thirty days a year to capture the spirit of these conversations, it is essential that we are front and centre with our communications during campaign. Equally important is our relationship with our audience outside of the campaign, choosing to only communicate when

spoken to, unless reporting on the outcomes of Movember funding. In considering real-time communications, Movember is also conscious of the quality and style of our communication choices. In this rapidly moving online world we have dedicated time to offline and personal communications such as handwritten thank-you cards for top fundraisers and framed [mementos].'

Similarly, can you describe the genius of the campaign?

'We believe that the genius of Movember is in its simplicity. It's the collective genius of our community who simply get involved by growing a Mo or supporting a man who does, that makes this work.'

MOVEMBER

significant challenges across all areas of the business, and creatively there is a local vs global trade-off as well as language and logistical challenges. Most important to Movember is that we continue to stay fresh and relevant in both established and new markets. The organizational goal is to move from successful to significant, and to be disruptive in how we operate, from the way we deliver the campaign to the way that we fund research though global collaboration.'

Have you been inspired by any other invented movements?

'The founding members of Movember have origins in the surfing and skating communities in Australia where strong values, rules, etiquette and passion were at the heart of everything. These brand-led movements inspired the Movember co-founders to create strong foundations and values for their own organization. Along the Movember journey numerous others have been an inspiration, including the breast cancer movement and Livestrong.'

What's next for Movember? What's the next creative hurdle?

'In one year, Movember has grown from fourteen countries in 2011 to twenty-one countries in 2012. This is in response to where we understand we have a following and supportive community. With this come

Can a digital movement save an analogue industry?

And now for a far trickier proposition: Can an online movement restore analogue music? Maybe. World Record Day was founded in 2008 as a way of getting people into record shops by staging in-store performances, events and exclusive new releases of music. The online element helps fans to locate their nearest independent record store, and to build a sense of solidarity. Previous Record Store Days brought about such oddities as a Feist/Mastodon mutual cover record ('Feistodon') and a limited-edition Flaming Lips album made with blood samples from the collaborators. Whether the internet can go from analogue music's greatest foe to its saviour remains questionable, but what has resulted is one of the calendar's most genuinely enjoyable branded days.

Ozioma Egwuonwu,
23 July 2012

A day for the hung-over?

Not so much about creating an event as grafting a hangover day onto a pre-existing one, 'Magnificent Monday' was created in protest. The Monday after Superbowl weekend is infamous for its rate of workers calling in sick (seven million on average per year), or showing up late and still under the weather (a further four million!)

Why not just call it a national sick day and leave us on our sofas? Coke Zero's campaign turned hung-over work-dodgers into 'activists' and rallied Twitter fans to make it a federal holiday, with the hashtag #magmonday.

The only way we could properly write a chapter such as this is to be involved in a movement ourselves. Jon met a fascinating woman called Ozioma Egwuonwu in New York, who was inventing a movement called the International Day for Dreamers. They had several brilliant conversations and even planned a South By Southwest Interactive talk about inventing movements. This planning process and observing Ozioma in action taught us a lot about what it takes to get a movement started and, more specifically, how to get people to take the wild ideas that pop up in your brain 'from dream to do'. That is what Urgent Genius is all about anyway, isn't it?

Using innovative tech to power a green movement

With the continued practice of Earth Hour, countries all around the globe look for interesting ways to raise awareness about its importance. Enter Tel Aviv's Earth Hour 2011 Web Cycle: the world's first website that works by pedalling a bike in real time. While riders pedal, the site stays on the air, but in a moment of pause, the site goes dark. The activity was broadcast on Earth Hour's website and on Ynet, Israel's leading website.

As a result, Earth Hour became the most-viewed website in Israel that day. Every three minutes, a new environmental tip was added to Earth Hour's website for millions to see.

'Held within a dream is hope for the future and held within each dreamer is a wealth of potential. DreamDay seeks to unlock the potential of the dreamer and by doing so transform the world.'

Ozioma Egwuonwu

Ozioma's a dream activist (great title) and motivational speaker and International Day for Dreamers is the first event of its kind. The challenge: In six weeks, get people to do something very counter-cultural: take an entire day just to dream while awake. Thanks to her hard work, the movement became a global one, with dreamers from more than twenty countries including Costa Rica, Australia, Uganda, Nigeria, Korea, Netherlands, UK, United States, Egypt, Indonesia, Poland, France and Ghana taking part.

How did the International Day for Dreamers come about?

'I was inspired by the Sarah Ban Breathnach quote "The world needs dreamers and the world needs doers. But above all, the world needs dreamers who do." I am an action-oriented person. Having the power to dream is only half the story. Providing the resources to put that dream in action is the most important part. That's what the International Day for Dreamers is all about. You have to be the change you want to see. By participating in DreamDay 2012, people are making history. This is the first time in history that people will collectively carve out time to co-create future possibilities across live and digital channels. On that day, people will make connections that crisscross the earth through the power of the visions they have for the future.'

What was the purpose of the day?

'The purpose of the day was not just to activate, or celebrate dreams, but to create an action plan on how to pursue those dreams, so you are not just a dreamer but a "DREAM RUNNER". While the celebration carves out time and space for participants to home in on what they truly desire, this is just the first step. The core of DreamDay 2012 turns wishful thinking into purposeful, organized action. We will activate the transformational power of dreams, goals and aspirations by empowering dreamers to do.'

Why 25 August? Any triggers in culture that point to this day as being the optimal day for dreaming?

'We picked the weekend before Labor Day on purpose. Every year, many countries around the world honour their ability to labour with labour holidays. This year, we want to honour the dreamer, the visionary, the innovator and the simple truth that before one labours, one must dream.'

What preparations have been made before the event? How will the day work?

'We have a team of influencers who have been spreading the word to their engaged communities. People were encouraged to download a "Dream Kit" [that contained] all the necessary content they needed to make the most of the day, including a Dream Declaration certificate where they could declare their dreams and share their aspirations with the world. We also created a great deal of visual inspiration to circulate throughout social channels. The day is all about dreaming and doing. It's about going to participating coffee shops and collaborating with a doer to come up with a plan for how to make things happen. Also, I will be giving a short live-streamed call to arms to inspire people to convert their dreams into actionable steps.'

Okay, it's time to stop dreaming and go out and invent an event. So you've got an idea you think people will gather around? Before you build your legion of like minds, consider the driving factors behind a few of the following movements. Then just go do it.

5

Patagonia's Cyber Monday

   Patagonia

Patagonia

USA

2011

We are living on a dying planet, and outdoor clothing company Patagonia let their feelings be known about it on Cyber Monday, the biggest online shopping day of the year in the United States (it grossed $1.25 billion in 2011). In true Urgent Genius style, they newsjacked the event to call out the 'culture of consumerism it reflects'. In a brilliant counter-cultural move, they emailed their customers to tell them NOT to buy their most popular item, a blue jacket made of 60 per cent recycled polyester, for environmental reasons. Although they couldn't stop Cyber Monday from happening, the idea got global attention, reducing Cyber Monday's carbon footprint and, ironically, eventually increasing Patagonia's sales by 30 per cent.

DON'T BUY THIS JACKET

It's Black Friday, the day in the year retail turns from red to black and starts to make real money. But Black Friday, and the culture of consumption it reflects, puts the economy of natural systems that support all life firmly in the red. We're now using the resources of one-and-a-half planets on our one and only planet.

Because Patagonia wants to be in business for a good long time – and leave a world inhabitable for our kids – we want to do the opposite of every other business today. We ask you to buy less and to reflect before you spend a dime on this jacket or anything else.

Environmental bankruptcy, as with corporate bankruptcy, can happen very slowly, then all of a sudden. This is what we face unless we slow down, then reverse the damage. We're running short on fresh water, topsoil, fisheries, wetlands – all our planet's natural systems and resources that support business, and life, including our own.

The environmental cost of everything we make is astonishing. Consider the R2® Jacket shown, one of our best sellers. To make it required 135 liters of

COMMON THREADS INITIATIVE

REDUCE
WE make useful gear that lasts a long time
YOU don't buy what you don't need

REPAIR
WE help you repair your Patagonia gear
YOU pledge to fix what's broken

REUSE
WE help find a home for Patagonia gear you no longer need
YOU sell or pass it on*

RECYCLE
WE will take back your Patagonia gear that is worn out
YOU pledge to keep your stuff out of the landfill and incinerator

REIMAGINE
TOGETHER we reimagine a world where we take only what nature can replace

water, enough to meet the daily needs (three glasses a day) of 45 people. Its journey from its origin as 60% recycled polyester to our Reno warehouse generated nearly 20 pounds of carbon dioxide, 24 times the weight of the finished product. This jacket left behind, on its way to Reno, two-thirds its weight in waste.

And this is a 60% recycled polyester jacket, knit and sewn to a high standard; it is exceptionally durable, so you won't have to replace it as often. And when it comes to the end of its useful life we'll take it back to recycle into a product of equal value. But, as is true of all the things we can make and you can buy, this jacket comes with an environmental cost higher than its price.

There is much to be done and plenty for us all to do. Don't buy what you don't need. Think twice before you buy anything. Go to patagonia.com/CommonThreads or scan the QR code below. Take the Common Threads Initiative pledge, and join us in the fifth "R," to reimagine a world where we take only what nature can replace.

patagonia
patagonia.com

*If you sell your used Patagonia product on eBay® and take the Common Threads Initiative pledge, we will co-list your product on patagonia.com for no additional charge.

TAKE THE PLEDGE

Because Patagonia wants to be in business for a good long time – and leave a world inhabitable for our kids – we want to do the opposite of every other business today.

National Cleavage Day

 Wonderbra

 Wonderbra

 South Africa

 2002 – present

This invented day is one that started before social media existed, but really came into its own when sharing photos online took off. The formula was simple: take one iconic brand, a nation of women and a subject guaranteed to turn heads. Let your campaign loose on social media, and let the eye candy, and PR like the article to the right, do the rest. Founded in South Africa in 2002, this 'invented holiday' recurs every April, inviting women to share cleavage photos online and celebrate girl power, while Wonderbra donate revenue from their sales to cancer charity The Sunflower Fund. It's since spread worldwide, especially over Twitter, where it trends globally on the day and has attracted saucy snaps from the likes of Beyoncé, Rihanna and Dita Von Teese. You had us at Beyoncé…sorry, what were we talking about?

One iconic brand and a nation of women sharing photos and turning heads.

Slurpee BYO
Cup Day

 7-Eleven Stores Australia

 Leo Burnetts Melbourne

 Australia

 September 2011

Ever wanted to slurp from a mannequin's cavity? Then head over to
7-Eleven on 'Bring Your Own Cup Day' and you can enjoy a Slurpee
from any vessel you want. In response to recent competition, 'BYO Cup
Day' was created to allow fans to go nuts with their favourite iced drink.
Using their substantial online following, they invited people to fill literally
anything they wanted for the price of a medium Slurpee. The results
were amazing – in just one day, sales increased 270 per cent, almost every
Slurpee machine ran dry and the fans created more content than in the
brand's entire history, uploading over thirty new photos and videos every
minute. Put that in your pipe and slurp it.

Slurpee belongs to its drinkers,
not 7-Eleven. Its attitude needs
to be as irreverent as
its drinkers.

National Day
of Unplugging

 Reboot

 Reboot

USA

March 2012

Every time Ashton Kutcher tweets, a publicist dies. So no wonder he 'took the pledge' and joined the National Day of Unplugging. Created by the Jewish art group Reboot, this 21st-century Sabbath is enjoyed by millions of people worldwide. The idea is simple. On Friday night, followers switch off all electronic devices until sundown on Saturday with the aim of using that time with friends, family or just themselves. For maximum impact, Reboot took their micro-digital-detox to the most logged-on place in the world: the South By Southwest interactive festival (SXSW). There they collaborated with RecordSetter (see page 176) to set the world record for the largest simultaneous cell phone switch-off. It just goes to show that with an act of Urgent Genius you can enjoy a slower pace of life in an instant. This event even encouraged co-author Jon to take two entire weeks off Twitter. He loved it.

An online movement
begging us to disconnect.

**Friend Me in
Real Life.**

Wanna hang out? I don't have a
computer or Facebook, but you
can look me in the eye, if you're
up for it.
#unplug

WWF Sweater Day

 WWF

 john st.

 Canada

February 2012

The Christmas jumpers your granny knits could save the world. Or so say WWF, who every February encourage Canadians to turn down the heat and put on a sweater. To spread the message of National Sweater Day, they hired agency john st., who created a grandma-centric campaign to communicate the message in a fun way. Users went online, chose from a range of grannies to call and got further information. They also booked a granny to call their friends. Thinking in an Urgent Genius way resulted in over one million people taking part, with the main sponsor, Loblaw, helping to reduce carbon emissions in their stores by nearly 530,000 kilograms over the year.

'A fun and easy way for Canadians to show that they value energy and want to use it wisely, not wastefully. '
Josh Laughren, WWF

Blue Monday's *The Good Times*

📢 Church of London

✍️ Church of London

📍 UK

🕐 January 2012

Mondays are miserable, but scientists decided to make our lives even more depressing by proving that a particular day in January is in fact the most depressing of the year, now known as Blue Monday. So the creative bods at Church of London decided to show some solidarity (and Urgent Genius) by creating, in only seven days, their own one-off newspaper *The Good Times*, of which they handed out 10,000 free copies on Blue Monday. It was filled with the best and happiest ideas from around the world, sought from people and organizations who give us all a reason to smile.

Good agency karma, distributed in print and online for free.

The Rally to Restore Sanity and/or Fear

 Comedy Central

 Comedy Central

 USA

 October 2010

When Comedy Central's satirists Stephen Colbert and Jon Stewart teamed up to spoof Glenn Beck, the United States's far-right conservative, they hit the jackpot. Their idea went viral almost instantly. Both comedians used their shows to create further buzz and intrigue, teasing the audience with potential guest speakers. What we learn here is that by newsjacking effectively, what may start as a minor prank can grow into something greater: a movement. Attendance of the rally was over 215,000, smashing the original estimate of 25,000, and it was even mentioned by President Obama. Whether it restored sanity and/or fear, we're not sure, but it certainly restored Comedy Central as a social-media-fuelled comedy juggernaut.

'If we amplify everything, we hear nothing.'
Jon Stewart

RALLY TO RESTORE SANITY AND/OR FEAR

10.30.10

WASHINGTON, D.C.

Movember

 Movember

 Movember

 International

 2003 – present

Every November, moustaches worldwide help to raise global awareness of men's health issues, particularly testicular and prostate cancer. Movember began in Melbourne, Australia, back in 2003 when thirty friends decided to get their Urgent Genius on and make charitable giving manly (and fun). By taking one of the strongest symbols of masculinity and hijacking it for a topic men hate to talk about, they managed to seriously change attitudes on an epic scale. Since its inception, 1.9 million Mos have been grown and £184 million has been raised globally, inspiring partnerships with the likes of Google and Qantas, who painted a giant Mo on one of their jets. Thanks to Movember, we'll never look at our upper lips or nether regions in the same way again.

STAND TALL
THE
Moustache
IS THE
MARK OF A MAN

HE IS A NATURAL BORN LEADER
HE STEPS UP AND LEADS WITH A CONFIDENCE OF BOTH
HIMSELF AND HIS SURROUNDINGS
HE IS SELFLESS AND BELIEVES LOOKING OUT FOR YOUR MATES
IS SOMETHING YOU DO NOT SOMETHING YOU MUST DO
HE IS ONLY CONTENT WHEN ALL ARE CONTENT
HE APPRECIATES THE LUXURY AND QUALITY OF CRAFTSMANSHIP
HE WOULD RATHER HAVE ONE UNIQUE HANDMADE PIECE
THAN ONE HUNDRED MASS PRODUCED ITEMS
HE IS DEDICATED AND TRUE TO THE CAUSE OF MOUSTACHERY
AWARE OF HIS RESPONSIBILITY TO HONOUR THE MOUSTACHE
HE LEADS A VALIANT LIFE WHETHER IT BE A SOLO ADVENTURE
INTO THE WILD OR A SIMPLE BBQ WITH FRIENDS
HE EXTRACTS AND REVELS IN WHAT LIFE HAS TO OFFER
A MAN WHO GROWS A MO KNOWS HOW TO ROCK
WHEN THAT TIME COMES HE LIKES HIS GOOD TIMES GREAT
WELCOME TO THE FAMILY

MOVEMBER
AND SONS

PURVEYORS OF KNOWLEDGE
& FINE MOUSTACHES

MOVEMBER.COM

Wear a Mo. Be a man.
And talk about it.

MOVEMBER AND SONS

STYLE GUIDE

The Rock Star

THE ROCK STAR IS BIG AND FULL OF ATTITUDE. NATURALLY NEAT AND WORN THE WORLD OVER BY COUNTLESS MUSIC LEGENDS.

The Undercover Brother

THIS UNASSUMING STYLE IS AN ESSENTIAL ADDITION TO ANY MOUSTACHE AFICIONADO'S TOOLBOX. JUST COVERING THE UPPER LIP WITH SUBTLY ROUNDED CORNERS, THE UNDERCOVER BROTHER IS THE PERFECT LOOK FOR THOSE WHO CRAVE A MO, BUT DON'T NEED UNDUE ATTENTION.

The Connoisseur

REMINISCENT OF VILLAINS, BRITISH INFANTRY AND DAPPER DETECTIVES, THE CONNOISSEUR IS PERHAPS THE MOST CLASSIC OF MO STYLES. THIS QUINTESSENTIAL MO IS EASILY RECOGNISABLE BY ITS ARTISTICALLY WAXED TIPS.

The Box Car

HANGING LIKE A SHAGGY INVERTED 'V' OVER THE UPPER LIP, THE BOX CAR IS AN IDEAL MO FOR NOVICES OFFERING MAXIMUM STYLE POINTS WITH MINIMUM UPKEEP.

The After Eight

EXTENDED LONG WAXED WHISKERS WHICH STRETCH OUT HORIZONTALLY LIKE THE LONDON BRIDGE. LOOSEN UP YOUR WAXING FINGERS AND GET READY FOR A TWIST.

The Regent

THIS MO STYLE IS FAMOUSLY WORN BY CENTURIES OF UPPER CLASS HUNGARIAN MEN. THE REGENT IS FIT FOR REVOLUTIONARIES AND OTHER BIG MOVERS AND SHAKERS.

Abrakadabra

ALSO KNOWN AS 'THE SURREALIST' THIS ABSURDLY STYLISH MO BLENDS ARISTOCRATIC ELEGANCE WITH ARTISTIC FLAIR.

The Trucker

THE FEARSOME TRUCKER BEGINS WITH A FULL BRUSH THAT HANGS LIKE A CROWBAR OVER THE UPPER LIP. MEANWHILE, THE ENDS PLUMMET DOWN TO THE BOTTOM OF THE CHIN FRAMING THE MOUTH IN A HORSESHOE ARC.

The Wisp

RECENT DECADES HAVE SEQUESTERED THIS STYLE TO THE REALM OF LOUNGE LIZARDS AND VEGAS HUSTLERS, BUT HISTORICALLY IT HAS BEEN HELD AS A MARK OF SOPHISTICATION.

PURVEYORS OF KNOWLEDGE & FINE MOUSTACHES

MOVEMBER.COM

Urgent Genius Cultural Calendar:

1. **International Beer Day – 5 August**
Country/Date of Origin: California, USA, 2007
Love of all things beer across fifty countries.
Hug a brewer and love the suds from every nation.

2. **World Sauntering Day – 19 June**
Country/Date of Origin: Michigan, USA, 1970s
Sauntering is not a walk, jog or run. It's aimless, happy strolling.
Tell your brand to slow down and master the saunter for a day.

3. **International Bacon Day – Saturday before Labor Day**
Country/Date of Origin: Massachusetts, USA, 2000
The world's most perfect meat needs its own day.
Bacon cookies? Bacon martinis? No rules. Any brand can apply.

4. **International Nurse's Day – 12 May**
Country/Date of Origin: Washington D.C., USA, 1953
A better day to celebrate nurses than Florence Nightingale's birthday.
How can your brand show some unsung health heroes some love?

5. **International Men's Day – 19 November**
Country/Date of Origin: Trinidad and Tobago, 1999
A day focusing on male health and positive male role models.
Does your brand appeal to men? Perfect. Capitalize on it.

A World of Unmissable Days and Events

6.

International Kissing Day – 6 July
Country of Origin: UK
Kissing as feel-good sport not social formality.
Full-on kissing's a full-on brand opportunity.

7.

International Dance Day – 29 April
Country/Date of Origin: Paris, France, 1982
Dance is a universal language.
Can you brand get its global groove on?

8.

World No Tobacco Day – 31 May
Country/Date of Origin: Switzerland, 1987
Global attention around the negative effects of smoking.
Incentivize customers to call it quits for a day.

9.

National Cleavage Day – 31 March
Country of Origin: South Africa, 2002
Celebrate the joys of the cleavage all for a good cause.
A legitimate reason for men to stare at boobs.

10.

World Toilet Day – 19 November
Country/Date of Origin: Singapore, 2011
Global commitment to improving sanitation conditions.
How can your brand build on the bog buzz this year?

'We want to fold hundreds of thousands of paper cranes and make wishes come true.'

Nina, six years old

6. Be genuine & relevant

Behind every screen there is a human writing the copy. Sometimes the best marketing of all is to let that humanity show or risk becoming a tool of our tools, as Thoreau says.

The lure of the trending wave can inspire brands to ride it out at all costs, even to their own detriment. For every story good-naturedly hijacked by a brand, there's another that turns out to be inappropriate, inauthentic and exploitative.

Case studies in this chapter demonstrate how important it is for brands to behave like human beings. Kind intentions and a sense of Urgent Genius equip people to overcome disaster, turning the tide by relying on social media, swift action and the old-fashioned spirit of invention to make a difference.

It's not good enough to be just human. You also need to use your brain and think about how your messages are relevant and appropriate for your audience at a specific moment in time.

We'll also explore what happens when things go horribly wrong (see pages 158–159). Poorly judged opportunism and commercial exploitation can destroy a brand in a day, while social media can play host to a lasting backlash. Let them serve as a warning: the Urgent Fails in this chapter should never be repeated.

If a brand wants to be more than two-dimensional and create an online dialogue with customers, it must be honest. Companies need to be confident of their own value and be prepared to give something back to followers for free. The thinking in question here is as much about

'Men have become the tools of their tools.'
Henry David Thoreau

maintaining a profile as it is about spontaneous acts. If you're a brand manager, it's critical that you think about the relevance of a story/event to your brand.

We've organized the case studies in this chapter around notable events. There are examples that tapped into the zeitgeist in a sympathetic and totally relevant way. There are others that take a sledge hammer to the proceedings and the subsequent collateral damage is significant. We cover several natural disasters and then lighten the tone with a tweeting snake and an American accidentally learning how to play cricket. We've also thrown in a mini-feature on crisis management. No one can be ignored. Your biggest PR disaster may lie in the hands of a three-year-old on a mission to change your product line.

....

Japanese earthquake of 2011

When a massive humanitarian disaster strikes, the commercial side of business seems insignificant. At 14.46 (Japan Standard Time) on 11 March 2011, Japan was hit by a devastating earthquake. A magnitude 9 quake off the Pacific coast triggered immense tsunami waves. 15,561 people were killed and over 125,000 buildings damaged. It was utterly devastating and the world was prompted into humanitarian action.

Google – Person Finder
Just an hour after the earthquake, Google's Crisis Response team launched a Japanese version of its Person Finder. The Person Finder made it possible for people to enter an enquiry about a missing person or provide information for interested parties. Google had launched a similar tool after the Chilean earthquake in February

2010. It was a speedy response, providing real utility to people in their time of need and making great use of Google's technology.

Zygna and Save the Children – Farmville
Next to react was Zygna, the world's number-one social gaming company. Zygna asked Farmville farmers to help the relief effort by making donations in the form of purchasing a permit to grow an exclusive daikon crop (see page 145). Within twelve hours of the disaster the crop was up and running. Zynga donated 100 per cent of proceeds to Save the Children's Earthquake emergency fund.

It was a brilliant value exchange. Save the Children received a cash injection (they raised over $1 million in the first thirty-six hours) and Farmers in Farmville had the ultimate badge of honour – a field of Daikon crops and a Japan relief flag.

 Megan Watt, Students Rebuild, December 2011

According to Japanese folklore, a wish may be granted to someone who folds one thousand origami cranes. Various individuals and organizations were inspired to create paper cranes as a symbol of support for Japan (see page 146). The most successful project made an amazing two million cranes from young people in over thirty-seven countries worldwide and all fifty U.S. states. A partnership was formed between Students Rebuild and DoSomething.org entitled 'Paper Cranes for Japan'. The original goal was 100,000 cranes, which would trigger a donation of $200,000 from the Bezos Family Foundation to fund Architecture for Humanity's

Sendai reconstruction efforts, in partnership with Japanese designers and builders. The organization then collaborated with artist Vik Muniz to capture the enormity of the project through photography and installations.

Could you explain how the idea came about?

'In response to the earthquake and resulting tsunami in Japan on March 11, Students Rebuild partnered with DoSomething.org's "Paper Cranes for Japan" campaign to inspire young people worldwide to support their Japanese peers. Because of the powerful symbolism of paper cranes – they represent hope, healing and recovery – it was the perfect call to action.'

How quickly did you get the initiative up and running?

'We sent out an Action Alert on March 17, six days after the earthquake struck. The Japan initiative was built for a quick call to action: the great combination of Students Rebuild partners and participants, the pre-existing infrastructure from Haiti Challenge, and social media made organized response nearly instantaneous. We quickly realized that we would have no problem meeting our 100,000-crane goal and instituted a postmark deadline: April 15.'

'There will be days when I walk in an arena and people will cheer and then there might be days when I walk in an arena and people might boo, but it all sounds the same to me because it's all just noise that lets me know that I'm relevant.'

Drake

Were you surprised by the response?

'Surprise would be an understatement. We were wowed, and also humbled. To illustrate: by April 11 we had counted 213,577 cranes. On April 14 alone we received 79,685 cranes. On April 19 literally hundreds of boxes arrived. On April 22 the count was 889,900. On April 26 the crane count reached one million! And we still had piles and piles of unopened boxes.'

Did you reach the fundraising target?

'Yes – in fact, we exceeded it. Our challenge to students was to make and mail in 100,000 cranes, which would trigger a $200,000 donation from the Bezos Family Foundation ($2 per crane). When the crane count exceeded the half-million mark, the foundation doubled its gift to $400,000 to reflect and further support all those who contributed to the campaign. Shortly after, an anonymous donor came forward to add $100,000, generating a total of $500,000 for Japan.'

The global examples we've just examined show how a collective humanitarian effort can make a massive difference. The individuals and organizations in the various projects all acted urgently to help a country in its time of need. Technology played its part in all of them. Social media helped connect millions in the various coordinated efforts.

Chilean mining accident

On 5 August 2010, thirty-three miners were trapped 2,300 ft (700 m) underground inside the Copiapó gold and copper mine in Chile after the shaft they were drilling in collapsed. They were rescued sixty-nine days later. After that amount

WHAT TYPE OF NEWS SHOULD YOUR BRAND NEWSJACK?

The news must have a relevant and genuine connection to your brand, of course. So let's chose a subject that's genuinely relevant to your co-authors to illustrate this point. As both of us have connections to British royalty*, we must open a chapter on being genuine with a story about Prince Harry. He had a bit of a wild time in Vegas and there were three responses that were both genuine and relevant, and demonstrate the point perfectly that what happens in Vegas with Prince Harry doesn't stay in Vegas. It gets him all over the tabloids and sets up some great newsjacking opportunities for relevant brands.

Top-three brands to newsjack the Prince Harry story

1. A cheeky lady-killing men's deodorant brand

A press ad on UrgentGenius.com from deodorant brand Lynx that stated, 'Sorry, Harry, if it had anything to do with us.' Lynx is known for its irreverent tone so the company can get away with associating itself with a slightly salacious story.

2. The hotel that Harry had his way in

Billionaire Vegas hotel owner Steve Wynn waived the £30,000 bill. This is classic newsjacking as a PR tactic. David Meerman Scott, in his brilliant e-book, Newsjacking, shows how these offers 'own the second paragraph' and help journalists have an interesting extra twist in the tale when they're writing about breaking news. While this isn't a creative execution, we mustn't ignore the power of hijacking the news as a way to get you noticed on urgent Google searches.

The porn industry

Vivid Entertainment honcho Steve Hirsch sent Buckingham Palace a letter offering Prince Harry $10 million to star in a big-budget porn film called The Trouble With Harry. We don't condone or encourage this sort of seedy newsjacking but it is an easy win when celebrities and sex are the main story drivers.

*Full disclosure:
Grant's a proper West Ham-supporting Englishman and Jon's lived in London for over a decade, and his brother-in-law has flown Kate and Will around in a helicopter. Proper British and royalty connections.

of time in near-pitch blackness, the miners' retinas needed protection from daylight.

Jonathan Franklin, a journalist at a Chilean media agency Addict Village was covering the news event. ACHS, the Chilean private health insurer, wanted to source some kind of eyewear protection for the miners when they surfaced. Franklin had a contact at Oakley, so he recommended the U.S. sunglasses manufacturer. Oakley donated thirty-five pairs of Radars that offered 100 per cent protection from the sun's UV rays. The miners wore them for a number of days after their rescue to allow their eyes to adapt slowly to life above ground. The Minister

of Mining, Laurence Golborne, also wore one of the extra pairs as a sign of solidarity.

At the time, CNBC maintained that in worldwide television impact alone, 'Oakley garnered $41 million in equivalent advertising time'. CNBC also reported on a degree of cynicism on Twitter. One person (@highlow) asked: 'Oakley is using the Chilean mine rescue as a marketing opportunity – poor taste or philanthropic move?' Another (@idaspeeda) called it 'the product placement of the year'.

On face value you could question Oakley's motives, but it's worth remembering that they were approached by the Chilean journalist and then donated them to the cause. The opportunity was presented to them and they grasped it. Eric Smallwood, vice-president of project management, told CNBC at the time: 'It's a goodwill gesture that will turn into mass amounts of exposure for Oakley in a positive manner.'

At the end of the day it was a win-win situation. Oakley helped save the eyes of thirty-three miners (a great product demonstration) and then benefited from the massive media attention from around the globe.

**@BronxZoosCobra,
14 July 2011**

On 26 March 2011, the Bronx Zoo, New York, had a bit of a situation: their Egyptian Cobra went missing. The Egyptian Cobra's venom is so deadly that it can kill a full-grown elephant in three hours. The New York media whipped up a bit of a frenzy, but reassurance came from an unexpected source as Twitter gave the snake a voice (see page 153). The reality of the situation was that the snake would be hiding, scared out of its tiny mind. The feed brought the snake and her adventures to life with a healthy dose of wit. The media changed its tune as they picked up on the positivity from people across New York who couldn't get enough of the cobra. To date

she has over 230,000 followers on Twitter. We chatted to social media's first snake socializer to find out a little more.

How did you manage the feed – was it a twenty-four hour operation?

They say that New York is the city that never sleeps, but its inhabitants definitely sleep in shifts. I found a few convenient places to hold up at night. One night the Hilton even gave me a suite. And it was. Sweet, that is.

And obviously, being a snake you must have had a human to help type your tweets?

This is the problem when a news channel like Animal Planet has humans running everything. There is a definite human bias. Just because a snake has no hands, nor fingers, nor feet, nor the proper documentation to obtain an iPhone, doesn't mean that an innovative snake can't make things happen. This is the city for dreaming big.

How quickly did you get 200,000 followers?

When I logged in on day two and had over 50,000 followers, I knew that New York City supports a strong, independent lady-snake about town. Within six days I had over 200,000. Sure, Charlie Sheen got over a million in

KID WRITES LETTER TO A BRAND: A MINI-CASE STUDY

This chapter ends with a Crisis Management Map outlining a few of our favourite Urgent Genius successes and failures related to brands' responses to topical events on social channels (see page 158). Preparing the map made us think about our favourite genuine and relevant brand responses. So here goes.

We want to discuss two letters – one written by an eight-year-old boy and the other by a three-year-old girl – which went viral on Twitter and Facebook. The response to the first is a massive FAIL. The response to the second is one that made us first smile and then think: 'Wouldn't it be great to offer this customer service manager a job as an Urgent Genius community manager?'

A bit of background: We help brands with their social channels every day, and we apply our Urgent Genius thinking to the way we manage our community managers, encouraging them to think proactively about how they can inject genuineness, relevance and, most importantly, personality and humour into their daily responses.

Letter One
Eight-year old Harry loves to draw planes, so he sent his latest drawing to Boeing to see if they'd consider building it for him. He got a form letter back saying that they had to return the letter because the company wasn't allowed to accept unsolicited designs because of intellectual property infringement issues.

The Urgent Genius in this case of Crayola Kid versus Jittery Jet Maker:

There were several examples. Harry received offers from two aviation museums. One even offered him the chance to host his own plane design show. A Boeing designer sent him information on plane design, but ultimately, the best example of Urgent Genius would have to be that of Todd Blecher, Boeing's Communications Director. He responded to the blog post from Harry's father Jon Winsor, asking the boy if he'd like to come on a tour of Boeing. The elder Winsor added, 'Todd gets it. Today, the best brands find ways to act more human, and Todd made Boeing more human. He's added value to the Boeing brand and showed that the company is willing to engage with consumers in a new way. His actions and attitude are the future of Boeing communications.'

Letter Two
In May 2011, Lily Robinson wrote a letter to supermarket chain Sainsbury's asking, 'Why is tiger bread called tiger bread? It should be called giraffe bread. Love from Lily Robinson, age 3 ½.' Chris King from the Sainsbury's customer services team wrote back: 'I think renaming tiger bread giraffe bread is a brilliant idea – it looks much more like the blotches on a giraffe than the stripes on a tiger, doesn't it?' He explained, 'It is called tiger bread because the first baker who made it a looong time ago thought it looked stripey like a tiger. Maybe they were a bit silly.' He included a £3 gift card, and signed the letter 'Chris King (age 27 & 1/3)'.

The Urgent Genius in this case of Blotchy Bread Girl versus Chris 'Customer Is' King:

For us, the real Urgent Genius was in Lily's mother. Sorry, Lily and Chris. She started a Facebook campaign to change the name of tiger bread to giraffe bread and had 14,000 shares. This prompted Sainsbury's to actually change the name to giraffe bread due to 'overwhelming customer feedback'.

one day and got in the *Guinness Book of Records* as the fastest-growing Twitter account, but he was already famous. And human. It is quite the honour. I feel like the snake equivalent of Justin Bieber.

Can a nickname as a Twitter handle get you a free trip around the world?

A Twitter username can quite easily create some unwanted attention. Ashley Kerekes of Westfield, Massachusetts, United States has the username 'theashes'. She took the name as her Twitter handle in 2007 because it was her boyfriend's nickname for her. She had no idea about cricket, let alone the biennial series between Australia and England. As the sixty-sixth Ashes series started in 2010, she started to attract a following from legions of passionate cricket fans. They bombarded her with messages and her initial response was to tweet 'I'M NOT A FREAKING CRICKET MATCH'. This

just made matters worse. Her initial following swelled from 300 to 7,000 in twenty-four hours.

In true Urgent Genius style, Qantas identified the opportunity and tweeted 'Qantas wants to see @theashes in Australia. We'll fly her from New York to Australia for the Ashes!' They then flew her out to the cricket-fest and garnered loads of media interest from the stunt.

While Qantas were sorting out her flight another brand jumped on the bandwagon. Vodafone set up a #teachtheashestheashes campaign so that cricket-savvy Twitter users could help explain the finer details of the sport to Ms Kerekes.

Keepin' it real: The vital importance of being genuine and authentic, as well as relevant. The following case studies bring these and other incredible examples to life.

'A squirrel dying in front of your house may be more relevant to your interests right now than people dying in Africa.'

Mark Zuckerberg

6

Daikon Crop

Lady Gaga buys $3 million worth of root veg. First, we had the meat dress. Now this? Presumably she was planning a vegetarian redress to her carnivorous PR stunt? No. She bought truckloads of the Japanese vegetable daikon on social game Farmville to raise money for the 100,000 children displaced in the Japan tsunami. Just twelve hours after the disaster, in a charitable act of über-Urgent Genius, Save The Children teamed up with social game-makers Zynga to create the virtual vegetable with 100 per cent of the proceeds going to the charity. Well done, Gaga and countless others for doing a bit of virtual good to help out in a real-life crisis.

Up and running in just twelve hours.

Paper Cranes
for Japan

 Bezos Family Foundation

 Students Rebuild

 USA

March – April 2011

According to Japanese legend, anyone who folds a thousand paper cranes will be granted a wish. When Japan was devastated by a tsunami, it needed more than a few wishes to come true. It also needed cash to rebuild. So Students Rebuild and DoSomething.org inspired students from thirty-eight different countries to fold two million origami birds. Every crane made and sent in to Bezos Family Foundation triggered a $2 donation to support the rebuilding efforts. Even globally acclaimed artist Vik Muniz got involved, creating a work of art using thousands of the origami cranes. This fine example shows that Urgent Genius isn't just about increasing sales. It's about mobilizing people with time on their hands to get crafty and use their art to change the world. Not a bad result for folding up a bit of paper, eh?

'On April 26 the crane count reached one million!'
Megan Watt, Students Rebuild

WATER MARK

JANUARY 2011

The Mark of Resilience.

This is the mark

that marks the

point where the floodwaters peaked.

The mark that marks

the day when the

iron will of ordinary people gave

to others when their

own lives were gutted.

The mark that marks the spirit in this

town and every town on

the hard road to recovery.

This is a day to mark in your memory.

When people came

and gathered together

had a drink, a laugh and kept going.

WATERMARK IS AN EVENT TO HELP STRENGTHEN THE SPIRIT OF QLD COMMUNITIES. IT WILL BE HELD IN 19 VENUES ACROSS REGIONAL QLD ON APRIL 16 FROM MIDDAY ONWARDS. VISIT THE WATERMARK TAB ON FACEBOOK.COM/BUNDYRUM FOR MORE. ATTEND THE WATERMARK NEAREST YOU AND SUPPORT THE QLD FLOOD RECOVERY.

Bundaberg
DISTILLING C°

Watermark Rum

 Diageo

 Leo Burnett

Australia

April 2011

When a region the size of France gets flooded, where do you find the courage to rebuild? In Queensland, Australia, you start at the brewery. Just two days after the January 2011 floods devastated their surroundings, the folks at Bundaberg Brewery got their Urgent Genius waterproof skates on, creating Watermark Rum to raise money for the recovery effort. Quickly becoming a national symbol of resilience, the limited-edition rum sold out in a week. But the quick thinking didn't stop there. The finale was The Watermark Music Festival, held simultaneously in sixteen of the worst-hit towns, proving that in Australia a natural disaster isn't reason to drown in self pity – it's a licence to act fast to help people and then kick back in grand style when the job's done.

'Uplift the spirits of communities...to bring a little joy back in time of great need.'

Matt Bruhn, Marketing Director, Bundaberg Brewery

HIPPO TRACKS INVENTORY THROUGH TWITTER.

@HelloMeHippo @HungerFighter Core Cell Local Distributor Retail Store

Plan-T

📢 Hippo Munchies

✍️ Creativeland Asia

📍 India

🕐 2011

Ever had the munchies and no Arabian salted snacks? Snack lovers, unite. This is a problem you can solve, thought ad agency Creativeland Asia. They helped Hippo Munchies fight hunger by launching Plan-T, a digital campaign that took on the challenge of Indian retail distribution by asking their followers to tweet when and where Hippo Munchies had sold out. This helped the brand track and prioritize demand so they could act on it immediately. It also helped them identify new markets. Within hours, they received messages from fifty cities, increasing sales by 76 per cent. Today, Plan-T is taught in business schools, published in marketing books and has been the subject of over 500,000 blogs and articles. Not a bad lesson to learn from what looks to us like a rice cake, albeit a very desirable one, evidently.

Hippo used his unique Hippo English to converse with his followers on Twitter.

 HelloMeHippo Hippo say dear all, Hippo happy and proud of you for fighting hunger. So inform Hippo of shop and location where You no see Hippo. Hug you:)
9.25 AM Mar 17th via web

 MumbaiCentral@HelloMeHippo Court canteens. Please. High Court. Sessions Court at Kalaghoda, Sewri and Dindoshi, and Magistrate Courts all over.
1:40 PM Mar 17th via Tweets60 in reply to HelloMeHippo

 HelloMeHippo Hippo get justice! Hippo come to court canteen soon. RT@MumbaiCentral Court canteens. High Court. Sessions Court and Magistrate Courts.
2:11 PM Mar 26th via web

 MumbaiCentral Woot! RT@HelloMeHippo Hippo happy to say Hippo soon coming to court canteens because you told Hippo. Hippo thank you for fighting hunger :)
2:18 PM Mar 26th via Tweets60

 Rrrrohini Ahmedabad!Gandhinagar! Hippo came n went. Retailers hungry it seems. RT @HelloMeHippo: Hippo feel bad that friends not find Hippo everywhere.
1.48 PM Mar 26th via TweetDeck

 HelloMeHippo Hippo say Hippo now there in sector 20 at Capital Parlour & many shops in sector 21-22 RT@Rrrrohini Gandhinagar! Retailers hungry it seems.
6.01 PM Mar 26th via web

 dootah@HelloMeHippo There no purple Hippo in Mahim W. No in Magnet supermarket. :(
11:26 AM Mar 15th via Chromed Bird in reply to HelloMeHippo

 HelloMeHippo Hippo now at Magnet and Mahim and ask where you are? RT@dootah@HelloMeHippo There is no purple Hippo in Mahim W. No in Magnet supermarket.
2:18 PM Mar 22nd via web

 dootah@HelloMeHippo Dootah thank hippo for bringing purple hippo to magnet store. Dootah not hungry anymore.
9:25 PM Mar 22nd via Chromed Bird in reply to HelloMeHippo

 dharmeshG @HelloMeHippo Hippo shortage in Lower Parel:I
2:12 PM Mar 26th via web in reply to HelloMeHippo

 HelloMeHippo Hippo say Hippo now available at Padamshri Dairy, Maya Ice Cream Parlor & Pathare PB Stores RT @dharmeshG Hippo shortage in Lower Parel:I
2:18 PM Mar 26th via web

 nicohla@HelloMeHippo Me want Hippo in Lower Parel, near Shri Ram Mills in the little dukaans.
1:57 PM Mar 22nd via web in reply to HelloMeHippo

 HelloMeHippo Hippo now at Shri Ram Mills! Masala stores, Padmashri Dairy, Maya Ice Cream Parlor & Pathare PB Stores RT @nicohla want Hippo in Lower Parel!
1:59 PM Mar 26th via web

The public became a Twitter-powered real-time sales force.

Lufthansa Open Letter

 Lufthansa

 Lufthansa

USA

2010

What's the worst ever way to get your boss to notice you? We call it the Gray Powell. He's the iPhone engineer who left a top-secret iPhone prototype in a German pub. By the next day, the secret was out. Lufthansa shared his pain (as well as his love of German beer), so they released an open letter, via Twitter, offering him a free business-class seat on one of their flights to Germany and access to their new Bavarian-themed lounges. By newsjacking the story in a truly genuine way, the German airline got as much PR as the original leak.

> 'iPhone loser gets free flight and beer from Lufthansa.'
> Mashable tweet

Lufthansa

April 21, 2010

Open letter

Dear Mr. Gray Powell,

I recently read in the news that you lost a very special phone at a German beer bar in California.

We all know how frustrating it can be to lose personal belongings, especially when it is such a unique item.

At Lufthansa we also noted with great interest your passion for German beer and culture.

We thought you could use a break soon -- and therefore would like to offer you complimentary Business Class transportation to Munich, where you can literally pick up where you last left off. Upon arrival in Munich, feel free to check out our new Bavarian Beer Garden Business Lounge, and experience the best that Germany has to offer.

We are looking forward to welcoming you on board.

Please contact my team via Twitter at www.twitter.com/Lufthansa_USA at your earliest convenience.

All the best,

Nicola C. Lange
Lufthansa German Airlines
Director Marketing & Customer Relations, The Americas

Golden Voice
Ted Williams

 Kraft

 CP+B

USA

 January 2011

Huge American food brand hires homeless ex-addict to voice-over their ad campaign. Now there's a PR angle that was sure to grab headlines. And that it did. Kraft's ad agency Crispin Porter + Bogusky hired Ted 'The-Man-With-The-Golden-Voice' Williams a few days after he'd been a surprise hit on YouTube thanks to a local journalist catching his amazing vocal gift on camera. Kraft hijacked a meme here in such a brilliant way that there was no backlash about Ted's past. They essentially gave him his first job in fourteen years, setting him on the road to recovery.

'Cheesy noodles topped with golden brown breadcrumbs – you know you love it.'

Ted Williams, Kraft Homestyle Mac and Cheese TV commercial

Bronx Zoo's
Missing Cobra

 Self-promotion

 @BronxZoosCobra

 USA

 March 2011

Bronx Zoo's Cobra
@BronxZoosCobra
I'm an Egyptian cobra back from being out on the town.
BronxZoosCobra@gmail.com
I'm at the Bronx Zoo. For now.

Bronx Zoo's Cobra @BronxZoosCobra · 30 Mar 11
Getting my morning coffee at the Mudtruck. Don't even talk to me until I've had my morning coffee. Seriously, don't. I'm venomous.
Expand

Bronx Zoo's Cobra @BronxZoosCobra · 29 Mar 11
City may not sleep, but I'm ready to. Ooh a chimney! I bet you bragged to your friends about having a working fireplace in NYC. Hi roomie.
Expand

Bronx Zoo's Cobra @BronxZoosCobra · 29 Mar 11
At Planet Rose in the East Village to get my karaoke on. Gonna sing some "White Snake." #snakeonthetown #likeadrifteriwasborntowalkalone
Expand

Bronx Zoo's Cobra @BronxZoosCobra · 29 Mar 11
Hey @piersmorgan, @jack and @biz, What does a snake have to do to get this account verified?
Expand

Bronx Zoo's Cobra @BronxZoosCobra · 29 Mar 11
Thinking about seeing "How to Succeed in Business Without Really Trying." That Daniel Radcliffe really speaks to me. #snakeonthetown
Expand

Bronx Zoo's Cobra @BronxZoosCobra · 29 Mar 11
Craigslist missed connection? RT @MikeBloomberg President Obama & I toured Museum of Natural History, saw 94ft whale but no @BronxZoosCobra
Expand

'I feel like the snake equivalent of Justin Bieber.'
@BronxZoosCobra

'There is no strict social-media policy for zoo animals', tweeted @BronxZoosCobra, the parody account that attracted over 200,000 followers in a week. The Urgent Genius trigger: an Egyptian Cobra escaping from the Bronx Zoo. As witty as the tweets were – 'Just FYI, I've had it with Samuel L. Jackson, too' – the real genius rested with the zoo's marketing team, who smartly allowed it to act as its first cold-blooded spokesperson, generating all the PR while they worked on finding the real reptile. Once they found the snake, the zoo asked users to name the detained escapee, reinvigorating the buzz and gathering 33,000 suggestions. We invited Mia the snake to join us on our panel at SXSW as the interactive festival's first ever reptile panellist.

4th Amendment Wear

📢 4th Amendment Wear

✍ Matt Ryan and Tim Geoghegan

📍 USA

🕐 2011

Going on holiday? No, sir. Not until you get naked in the airport for some strangers. As the controversy surrounding full-body scanners was trending online, Crispin Porter + Bogusky creatives Matt Ryan and Tim Geoghegan experienced the joys of being electro-violated first-hand. Their response was both urgent and genius. Citing the U.S. Constitution's Fourth Amendment, which guards against unreasonable searches, they created a T-shirt label that has the words of the amendment written on each shirt with a unique metallic ink that shows up on scans. Their timing was perfect as well. They launched their shirts on Thanksgiving, the United States's busiest travel period. With a tiny budget and a smart use of social media, they got on every major news channel, winning Cannes Gold along the way.

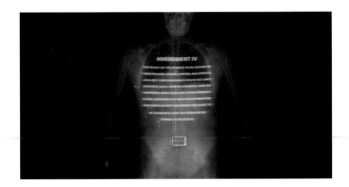

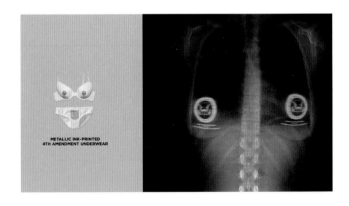

1,205,389 hits on the weekend of launch.

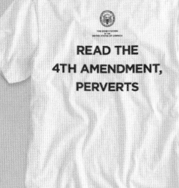

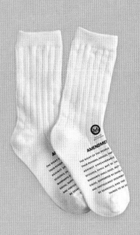

CURATORS
OF SWEDEN

I'M @Sweden

Curators
of Sweden

 Swedish Institute and Visit Sweden

 Volontaire

Sweden

December 2011 – present

This Swedish government-backed venture put the national Twitter account in the hands of its citizens for one week each, without censoring a single character. Curators of Sweden promoted Sweden as the democratic, diverse and exciting place it is. And its effect was both Urgent and Genius, as retweets and replies shot up 553 per cent, gaining new followers from over 120 different countries. In addition, @Sweden trended globally, inspiring other governments to create their own national accounts. This was an important demonstration of the positive power of social media.

There is no censorship and not a single tweet has been removed.

Crisis Management Map: A World

1. USA: A Smart reply

In June 2012, Clayton Hove, an outspoken ad critic in the United States, took a swipe at Smart with the following remark on Twitter: 'Saw a bird had crapped on a Smart Car. Totaled it.' There are many examples of brands either turning a blind eye or descending into paranoid over-reaction to comments on social channels. Smart USA lived up to their name with their brilliant response, an infographic that showed how much pigeon poop the car could actually take, along with the following tweet: 'Couldn't have been one bird, @adtothebone. Sounds more like 4.5 million. (Seriously, we did the math.) pic.twitter. com/aLYScFR3'.

2. France: La Redoute faux pas

La Redoute, the French fashion retailer generated some inadvertent buzz in January 2012. They had to remove a picture from their site that featured four child models clad in La Redoute, unaware that there was a nudist in the background. It took only four hours for their online community to spot the error after it was posted on the La Redoute site. With the storm brewing, the French fashion retailer didn't bury its head in the sand. They came out fighting and tackled the issue head on. They devised a speedy response involving a further fourteen fake fails hidden in the 33,000+ images on the retailer's site. Dinosaurs and meteorites amongst other things were Photoshopped into images for people to find. By finding the images, visitors were in the running to win a head-to-toe makeover courtesy of La Redoute. In less than forty-eight hours, all of the doctored images had been discovered and the online chat turned positive as people complemented the company for embracing the mistake. In the face of adversity, La Redoute had wrestled back its reputation and benefited from over $1 million worth of earned media.

Urgent Fails and Genius Recoveries

3. Germany: Mini Cooper Cold Front

As we all know, the weather can be an unpredictable beast so to rely on it in any way is a risk. Queen Elizabeth's Diamond Jubilee bears testimony to that. But it's not just the UK that suffers from ever-rubbish weather. In Germany, you can sponsor a high or low weather front and give it a name as well. Germany's meteorology institute's Aktion Wetterpate 'Adopt a Vortex' scheme has been running since November 2002. All you need is €199 for a LOW pressure system and €299 for a HIGH pressure one. The guys at Mini jumped on this and bought the rights to the third high-pressure front of the year in 2012. They named it Cooper, after their new Mini Cooper Roadster. Positioned as a wind- and weatherproof idea, it tied in with their advertising campaign 'Mini makes the weather'. Unfortunately the front brought some of the coldest weather Europe had seen for years. Temperatures dropped to -33°C (-27.4°F) and 113 people died. In an attempt to tap into the weather in real time, this stunt backfired and BMW had to issue a statement of regret.

4. Thailand: KFC Facebook alert

In April 2012, tsunami alerts were issued in Indonesia, Thailand and surrounding countries after an earthquake measuring 8.6 on the Richter scale hit the coast of Sumatra. KFC Thailand posted the following message on their wall: **'Let's hurry home and follow the earthquake news and don't forget to order your favourite KFC menu.'**

It encouraged Thais to leg it home to check out the earthquake news and suggested that they grab a promotional bucket of the Colonel's finest on the way. Unsurprisingly the internet backlash was intense and resulted in the global press picking up the story. KFC removed the message swiftly and replaced it with a new post that asked for forgiveness for the insensitive nature of the remark. It was reported that the apology message received over 100 comments and 700 likes. It goes to show that if you make a mistake and act like a human being, you can limit the damage. Of course, we recommend always thinking through the variables before diving into a newsjacking opportunity.

'...a 24-hour, non-stop challenge. A new story, a new designer and a new t-shirt everyday.'

Georgia Dixon, MITN

7. Create a platform

As we wrote in the 'Plan your spontaneity' chapter (see page 64), sometimes it's best to set the stage for Urgent Genius to give it a better chance of success. UrgentGenius.com is a stage in itself – a platform to attract followers, showcase their work and gradually build an online movement.

Platforms like Orange's The Feed (see page 172) or the 30 Days of Creativity blog (see page 169) have a distinct advantage over regular campaigns. They last longer, renewing their own online buzz with every successful addition to the site. They build communities around a cause. Because they feature constantly updated creative content, they have the chance to be topical again and again. People need these constant reminders. They miss the first five bits of genius you create because they're busy and their heads were in a different space. If you're going to engage them on a trending topic they're already discussing online, you're going to have to make sure you get in there quick with something that's

easy to digest and share. However, the holy grail for your platform is that it is ideally all three of the following:

1. Hugely Entertaining and/or So Surprising That I Must Share
2. Easy to Share
3. Easy to Interact With and Create a Personalized Response

As you'll find out shortly, it can still be a platform if it has only two of these three requirements. But the ones that are poised for greatness have all three.

If all these objectives are met, then the chance of building deep, ongoing relationships is great. Of course, this leads to engaged brand advocates who have the potential to influence online conversations. They can become your greatest ambassadors provided you give them content that has true value. In this chapter, we'll look at various brands and individuals who have

CREATE YOUR PERSONAL PLATFORM

What does 'create a platform' really mean? Two things. Firstly, it's about creating interactive spaces for brands. We've already discussed those types a bit. The second type of platform is your own – your personal launch pad. This is crucial if you're going to bring extra eyeballs to your Urgent Genius creations.

Hopefully, if you've read this chapter in order, it's all about what you create for brands – little self-contained fortresses that house content that people will interact with, chop, change and make their own before sharing it with their little tribes of like minds. Then what? What's the point of spending forty-eight hours without sleep (as you'll find out in the next chapter about the Urgent Genius Weekender) if you haven't developed your own platform to amplify it? We've tucked into a bit of brand platform goodness, so now it's time for a lucky bonus (it is chapter SEVEN after all). Here are a few tips on how to make sure that your own personal platform is in place to give your content an extended life.

Michael Hyatt in his aptly titled book, Platform, spends 200+ pages talking about this, and we recommend that you read it. This is how he defines a personal platform:

'Your platform is the means by which you connect with your existing and potential fans. It might include your company website, a blog, your Twitter and Facebook accounts, an online video show, or a podcast. It may also include your personal appearances as a public speaker, musician, or entertainer. It might even include traditional media such as a newspaper column, magazine articles or radio show. It most likely will include a combination of all these items. In order for you to be successful in today's business environment, you need two things: a compelling product and a significant platform.'

Michael's conclusion was: focus on the platforms that can't be taken away from you. Twitter and Facebook are important as PR tools for sure. But the most effective launch pad for your upcoming series of Urgent Genius experiments is of course your own personal blog. Guilty as charged. By the time you read this, we will have totally revamped UrgentGenius.com and our house will be in order so you can have a fresh digital injection of new mind-blowing stuff. Take a quick break from your bath (we assume this is bubble-bath reading, right?) and check out our new digs using any QR code in this book – assuming you take your smart phone with you when you're in the bath. That's the very nature of our site, or our platform if you will.

So wait, if you don't really read blocks of text usually, let us bullet point the way for you. Let's end on three compelling bullets that hopefully will hit you right in between the eyes. We'll even give it an over-the-top title in the style of an attention-getting infomercial:

Three Reasons Why You Need To Build Your Personal Platform Right Here, Right Now Or Your Money Back And Keep The Free Gift:

1. Visibility
People will be able to find you more easily.

2. Amplification
Your readers will share your content and help you grow your community.

3. Connection
You can engage in two-way conversations (e.g. on Twitter or in comments.

invested time and effort to constantly surprise and delight their community. By doing this, they get a significant return in the form of earned media that is impossible to buy (well, you can buy clicks and views, but they aren't the deep and meaningful interactions that we'll explore over the next few pages).

Jon Plackett, The Artistifier
22 July 2012

Created in the interim between BAFTAS win and Oscar glory of *The Artist* (the film was a trending topic, going on to take five Academy Awards), The Artistifier is a YouTube platform allowing users to turn any video clip into an 'award-winning film' with a set of online tools (see page 170). Films became grayscale and silent, soundtracked with piano and punctuated with black subtitle cards. 14,000 films were 'Artistified' within a week of launching, including 'Transformers', which was reworked to genius effect a few days later on Comedy Central's *The Colbert Report.*

Talk us through the genesis of The Artistifier.

'We had been chatting for a while about the power of real-time creativity and wanted to make something together. Often advertising is like turning up at a party and only wanting to talk about your own collection of stamps. To make something viral (or make friends at a party) it's a lot easier if you talk about what everyone else is already talking about – but add something new to the conversation. We saw that the Oscars were coming up and took a punt on *The Artist* winning. If it did, we knew that for at least forty-eight hours everyone on the planet would be talking about it.'

How does The Artistifier work specifically?

'We hit upon the idea of 'Artistifying' YouTube videos: making them black and white, flickery and orchestrally scored, and letting people add subtitles. It works in a similar, but more interactive way, to the Hitler *Downfall* remixes. It had to be quick and easy to use, but precise enough to craft something if you wanted to put the effort in.'

How did you launch it?

'We launched The Artistifier at a live social-media comedy event, where we re-imagined the audience's worst films as artistic masterpieces. In its first ten days, The Artistifier has been visited by 120,000 people, who've created over 12,000 Artistified films.'

A community of phone users rewarded by their provider with little touches of sweetness. We've already talked about The Feed in Chapter 3 (see page 73). We specifically looked at their Valentine's Day work but The Feed was so much more than a single idea; rather, it was a place to click on when bored or creatively frustrated, an interactive platform that always surprised and delighted the visitor (see page 172).

An ambitious undertaking for Orange, The Feed offered topical games, polls and interactive fun. 'Greatest Hits' from The Feed included illustrated Valentines tweets, commemorative plates for the public (in response to the Royal Wedding) and a photo generator that allowed users to turn themselves into superheroes. After eighteen months and thousands of personalized animations, plates, voice overs, profile pictures and many more surprises, the adventure came to an end. We think it's one of the best examples of a sustained effort to deliver real-time responses that delight over the long term.

How did the campaign work? Did the artists get to choose which material to animate?

'We were given guidelines on the Orange "endslate" that appears in each animation; other than that we were free to produce the animations as we saw fit. Tom negotiated what would be possible; two animations would be delivered each day of the week, with two animation directors.'

How Urgent was the operation?

'The crux of the job was spontaneity. During a day, two tweets would come in, be animated, edited and have the sound mixed so the finished films could be delivered the same evening.'

Do you think keeping things short-form is the way forward?

'Attention spans for web-based advertising and film are short purely because there's so much to look at. If something bores you, even slightly, you click on to the next thing. The video also streams faster if it's smaller so people don't have to wait for it to load. So yes, I believe that for web-based virals, keeping things short is the way to go.'

'It's what you do that makes you who you are and how you project that to others that makes you memorable.'

Dan Schawbel, blogger/personal branding expert

Georgia Dixon, Made in the Now,
19 June 2011

Made in the Now is a different type of platform that challenges creatives to produce an original T-shirt design related to the day's news (see page 180).

Made in the Now is an online T-shirt design studio and retail store. It launched in mid-2011 and they create a new T-shirt every twenty-four hours, based on a news story that has broken in that time. The site invites each visitor to vote on newsworthy topics, then a designer is commissioned to turn the chosen story into a limited-edition T-shirt design. The shirts are only available for a twenty-four-hour period, making them highly collectable. The Made in the Now project really embraces the speed of the web and plays with today's trend for fast and disposable fashion. The geniuses behind the project are two of the members of Brisbane-based design studio Josephmark.

How did Made in the Now come about?

'Made in the Now (MITN) launched as a peaceful protest against what we saw as increasingly unfortunate hallmarks of the fashion industry – derivative design, mass consumption and irresponsible production. Our thoughtful, timely tees are created locally and to order, which means there's no wastage, and each tee is sent out in sustainable packaging.'

Can you talk us through how the submission process works and how the news story gets selected?

'Every morning, fans of MITN can vote via Facebook for the story they most want to see on that day's tee. The designer then has less than four hours to come up with a concept and create a covetable design. The end result goes live every day at 2.00 p.m. (Brisbane, Australia time).'

What challenges have you faced with the real-time nature of the project?

'MITN is a twenty-four-hour, non-stop challenge. A new story, a new designer and a new T-shirt every single day gets the blood pumping – which is just another reason why we love it. We work across time zones, which means designers are often sweating in the small hours to come up with a wearable concept. In a project where time is everything, MITN turns fast fashion on its head.'

How do you source the illustrators?

'As advocates of considered, masterful design, we collaborate with a pool of handpicked designers and illustrators dotted across the world. Not only do we search for news each day, but we also scour the web for designers and invite them to join our community. Banding together on a thrilling challenge is a lot of fun! So far, MITN has utilized design talent from the UK, Australia, Argentina, Germany, France, Sweden, Poland, New Zealand, the Dominican Republic, the United States and Canada.'

Which design has been the most popular?

'Steve Jobs passing away is one of our most popular shirts to date, and also one of our most controversial. For those unfamiliar with our concept, it can take some getting used to why and how we do what we do, and some people were uncomfortable with us selling a T-shirt tribute to him immediately following his death. Our role is to present topical stories every single day, so when a beloved genius departs, it's more than likely going to make our news poll. The fans voted for Jobs, and in response, the designer created a very fitting tribute tee.'

 Kevin McGlade, iris worldwide 20 July 2012

To promote the control benefits of the new Predator football boot, iris London created the 'Call the shots' campaign (see page 178). Everyone was invited to go online and suggest challenges or activities for the best players in the world. Suggestions ranged from the grand to the bizarre. The real-time leader board showcased the ideas, which moved up and down according to how many votes they received.

To drive online conversations, the iris team responded to some of the posted requests. Midway through the campaign, the team turned up at Manchester United's training session with a camera, and Dimitar Berbatov and Nani took on some of the challenges. One request was for Berbatov to do a *Godfather* impression and Dimitar delivered. The YouTube clip garnered 300,000+ views in a week.

The top fifty submissions at the end of the voting each won tickets to attend an exclusive event at the Truman Brewery, London, on 18 May, where the likes of Van Persie, Kaka and other adidas stars undertook other challenges.

How did the idea come about?

'We saw this as the perfect example for how Urgent Genius can amplify existing campaigns. Our agency had already been given the task of running the boot launch. We just made sure

that we maximized all opportunities to use what people were talking about online as fodder to increase traffic to the campaign. So we were a bit scrappy on set. We took Berbatov and Nani aside for five minutes and made a few quick films that we knew would help drive traffic to the campaign.'

What did you do specifically? And how was it Urgent Genius?

'We looked at what the buzz was online around the campaign and around stars on the shoot. We picked the best ideas that we felt would maximize the pre-existing buzz as well as what triggers would accelerate the campaign. Berbatov had been in the news recently so we

homed in on him as our main target. We then trawled through all the fan-submitted ideas looking to find the suggestion that we felt Berbatov could pull off the best. The *Godfather* impression was perfect.

With the Nani suggestion, we knew that getting him to act out the fans' most popular submission – kicking footballs at someone's back side, which was suggested by over fifty different people – would be very shareable with the Call the Shots community and young football fans worldwide.'

So if you're ready, we're about to throw several platforms at you in quick succession. Would they charm you into sharing or interacting with them? Creating personalized platforms for brands and people – this is the future, so be sure to check out UrgentGenius.com for several more recent examples.

'A platform means that you don't have to get past the gatekeepers or spend thousands of dollars on advertising in order to have an audience.'

Michael Hyatt, *Platform*

7

30 Days of Creativity

📢 30 Days of Creativity

✍ Carmichael Lynch

📍 USA

🕐 2010 – present

Urgent Genius is about channelling your inner Swoosh and 'just doing it'. That's why we love ad-agency Carmichael Lynch's '30 Days of Creativity' initiative. It challenges you to make something every day for all thirty days in June, serving as a motivational tool for people to tackle their artsy to-do lists. It's been a global hit for nearly six years now despite the fact that there's no prize. Okay, if you have to have a prize, go to Melbourne. A selection of work is made into a film and exhibited at a gallery there.

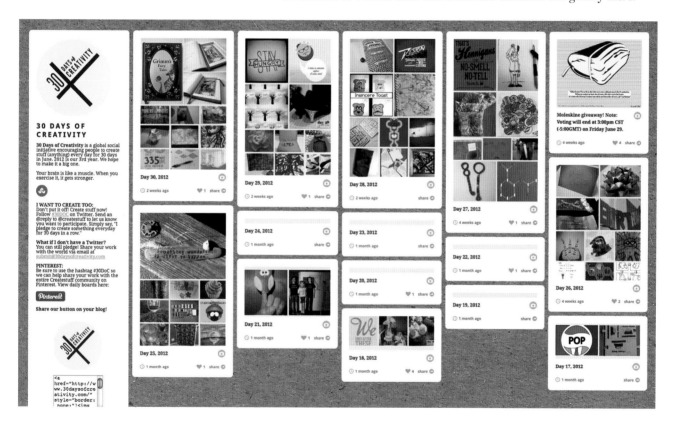

Your brain is like a muscle. When you exercise it, it gets stronger.

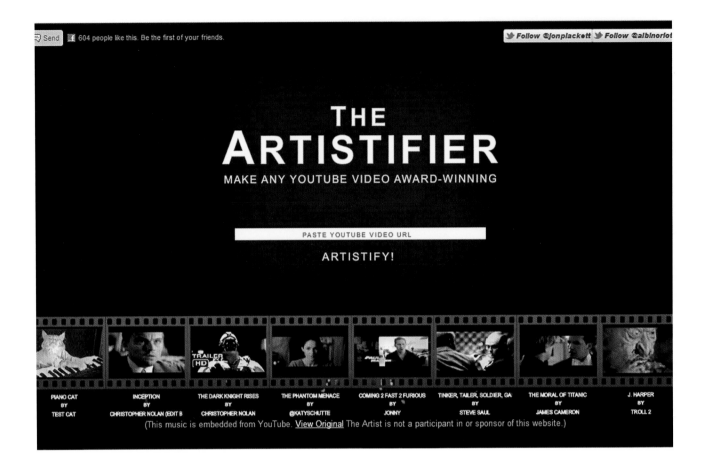

(This music is embedded from YouTube. View Original The Artist is not a participant in or sponsor of this website.)

The Artistifier

📢 Self-promotion

✍ iris worldwide and Bt33

📍 UK

🕐 February 2012

How do you create 14,000 award-winning films in a week? Easy. Build an interactive platform and adopt a very loose definition of 'award-winning'. With a Hollywood elevator pitch of 'Turn any video into an award-winning film in seconds', The Artistifier was simple – you enter a YouTube link and it plays it back in black and white with a 1920s soundtrack and your own funny captions. Led by co-author Jon and Jon Plackett, the site was timed perfectly, launching a few days before *The Artist* won best picture at The Oscars. A site that turns cat videos and bad movies into silent films AND tests your comedy writing skills? What's not to love?

14,000 films were Artistified within a week, riding the wave of Oscar buzz.

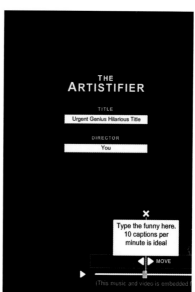

The Feed

Orange

Poke London

UK

2010 – 2012

Wasting time on the internet is easy. Turning those distractions into an award-winning platform that rewards simple participation is hard. For eighteen months, 'The Feed' featured forty-six mini campaigns that helped launch offers, products and deals. It also included topical experiments like an Easter egg-hatching competition and animating Valentines' Day tweets (see page 73). No big shock here: The platform grew Orange's social community and was a huge hit online.

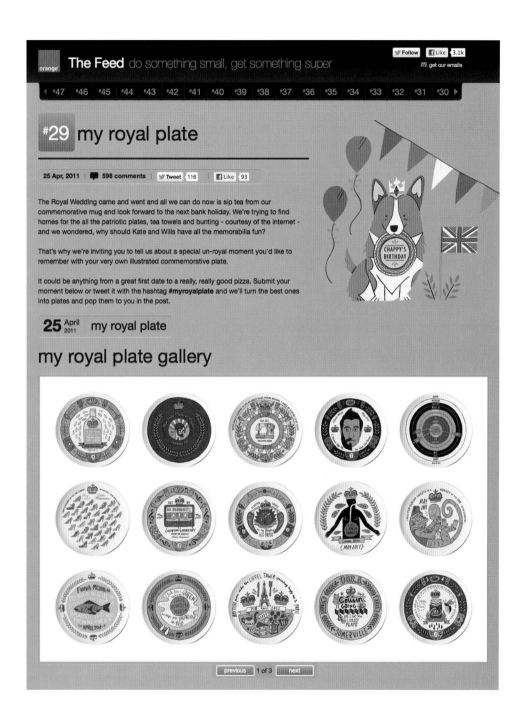

Do something small, get something super.

CNN.com
Mar. 7th 2011
Eastern cougar
declared extinct,
confirming decades
of suspicion

F*ck Yeah Headlines

 Eric Wedum

 F*ck Yeah Headlines

 USA

January 2011 – present

In an age when nothing surprise anyone any more, a forty-foot woman, made of stone, crushing a man walking his dog would surely turn a few heads. That's how Denver-based interactive-illustrator Eric Wedum envisioned the *Beacon News* headline 'Big Rock Woman Accused of Murder'. Eric searches various news sites and illustrates his favourite headline every few days without reading a single word of the article. F*ck Yeah Headlines started humbly, but after being picked up on Reddit it now boasts over 100,000 hits a day and was chosen as one of Thrillist's favourite websites of 2011. It's become so popular that Eric is thinking of expanding the blog to illustrations of celebrity tweets. Eric, you are the future of Urgent Genius.

> 'Finding the right headlines is key.'
> Eric Wedum

RecordSetter

 RecordSetter

 RecordSetter

 USA

2004 – present

How many blueberries can you fit in your belly-button? It's questions like this that RecordSetter was created to answer. Records are entered via video uploads and approved by both the community and the RecordSetter Council. Since its creation as a Burning Man project in 2004, thousands of records have been entered and RecordSetter has even landed a recurring segment on *Late Night With Jimmy Fallon*. Surely that's a record in itself?

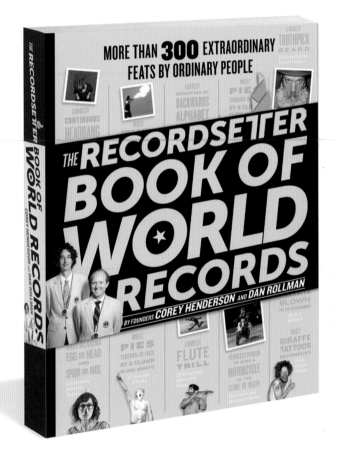

An online network of obscure, ridiculous and extraordinary achievements.

RecordSetter By The Numbers

A glimpse at some top world records of 2011 from RecordSetter.com, the new home of world records.

RECORD SETTER

World Records By Country

Top 5 Countries

Which countries set the most RecordSetter World Records?

- **690** Canada
- **93** Turkey
- **107** India
- **4,445** United States
- **97** Australia

Top Countries Per Capita

How many RecordSetter World Records set per million people?

26.63 per million	18.19 per million	5.97 per million	4.87 per million	4.74 per million
Canada	United States	Australia	Philippines	Switzerland

Social Media World Records

- Most Pending Facebook Friend Requests: 3,006
- Most Comments On A Facebook Wall Post: 59,380
- Most Notes On A Tumblr Post: 4,773,243

Celebrity World Records

Justin Bieber
Most Tweets Sent During A Live Interview
29 Tweets

Andrew W.K.
Most Times Singing The Word "Party" In A Song
204 Times

Kobayashi
Most Turkey Eaten In 10 Minutes
7.5 Pounds

Jimmy Fallon
Most Fast Food Items Tasted In 30 Seconds
13 Items

Physical Achievements

- **Fastest Time To Eat a Lightbulb** 33.86 Seconds
- **Longest Headspin** 13 Minutes, 53.34 Seconds
- **Most Swords Swallowed in 30 Seconds** 6 Swords
- **Loudest High Five** 87.1 Decibels
- **Fastest 400-Meter Dash While Juggling** 56.23 Seconds
- **Most Skateboards Ridden at Once** 3 Skateboards
- **Most Boob Wiggles in 30 Seconds** 68 Wiggles
- **Heaviest Vehicle Pulled with Beard While on Rollerskates** 1,046 Kilograms

World Record Partnerships

TOYOTA
World Records Set By Toyota Prius in 48 Hours
200+ Records

LIVESTRONG
World Records Set By LIVESTRONG to Raise Cancer Awareness
100+ Records

Stride
World Records Set By Stride Gum Facebook Fans
1,300+ Records

Gaming World Records

Angry Birds
Combined Total of all Angry Birds Record Attempts
58,827,710 Points

Words With Friends

Highest Single Move Score on Words With Friends
1,672 Points

O x y p h e n b u t a z o n e

2011 was RecordSetter's biggest year ever, with world records submitted from over 50 countries. Want to be the world's best at something? Visit RecordSetter.com today.

RECORD SETTER

Learn more about these records:
recordsetter.com/infographic

11,000+
Total records set

6,500+
Records set in 2011

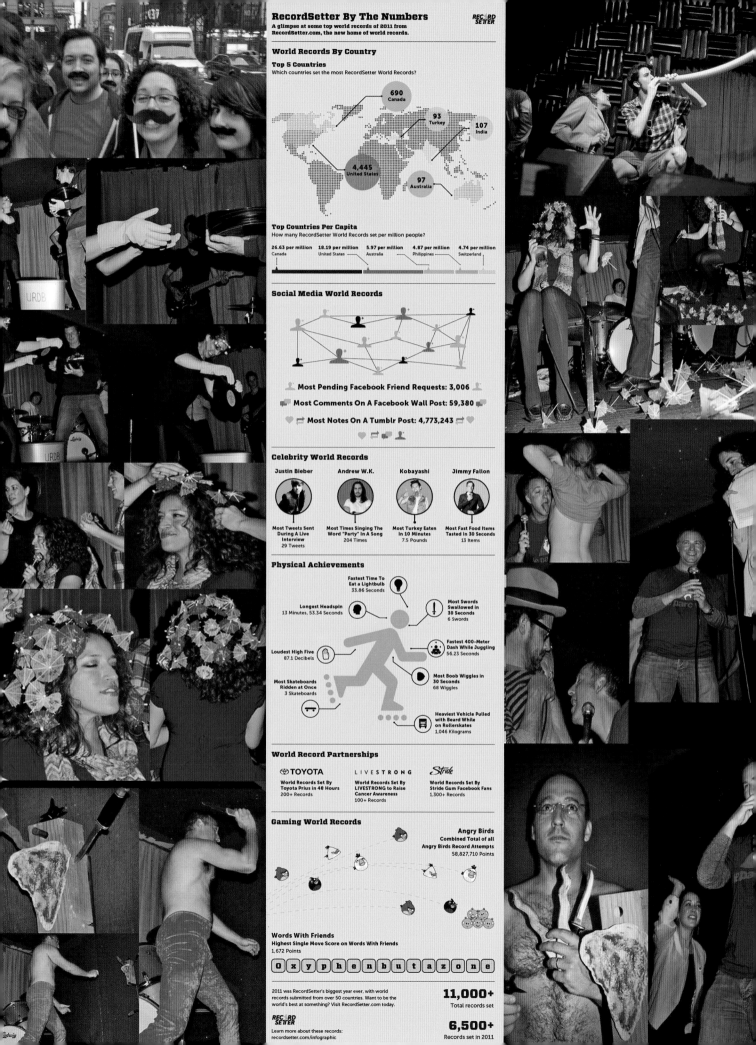

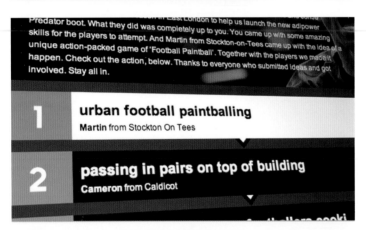

Call the Shots

adidas

iris worldwide

UK

May 2011

To celebrate the total control of the new adiPower Predators, adidas and ad agency iris worldwide (including co-author Jon) gave fans an interactive platform where they had 'total control' over football stars, including Manchester United's Nani and Dimitar Berbatov. As suggestions streamed in, the agency singled in on what teenage boys would want – Nani kicking footballs at a target placed on someone's back side and Dimitar doing a brilliant *Godfather* impression (in response to online chat about him looking like the Godfather). The videos were launched right before the Royal Wedding in the hope that boys would be Royal-ly bored and on YouTube. The videos clocked almost 500,000 views. Urgent Genius HQ: 1. Royal Wedding: 0. Sometimes, it's all about realizing who's not interested in a big, trending event and then kicking ass to get them what they want.

Asking the crowd to call the shots.

TIME LEFT

00 59 59
/HRS /MINS /SECS

NO.78
WALL STREET PROTESTERS. WE'RE IN FOR THE LONG HAUL

The protesters who have been camping out in Manhattan's Financial District for more than two weeks eat donated food and keep their laptops running with a portable gas-powered generator. They have a newspaper - the Occupied Wall Street Journal - and a makeshift hospital.

Read more | Forbes, 03.10.11

QTY	SEX	SIZE	[+]
TOTAL		AUD	**$40.00**

BUY THIS DESIGN NOW »

Like < 54   Tweet < 1

DESIGN BY The Hungry Workshop

DOWNLOAD THE FREE APP FOR IPHONE

JOIN US ON FACEBOOK

© Made in the Now 2012 | About | FAQ | Terms | Size Chart | Shipping | Download the app | Media

Sign-up for e-news   »   Follow us:

'Every day, MITN produces a collectable T-shirt
in response to a breaking news story.'

Georgia Dixon, MITN

Made in the Now

📢 Made in the Now

✒ Made in the Now

📍 Australia

🕐 2011 – present

'Desmond Tutu calls for Blair and Bush to be tried over Iraq.' That was the headline fans of 'Made In The Now' voted for as that week's most-wanted design. Every seven days, the small Brisbane-based company newsjacks the latest headlines by printing them on T-shirts. Customers across the world vote for their favourite story on Facebook. The most-liked one is sent off to a designer, who has a deadline of only three-and-a-half hours. We've selected a few of our favourites for events like Occupy Wall Street (above), the death of Beastie Boys' MCA and a random news story where a cat fell nineteen floors unharmed, hence the 'SpiderKitty' design (opposite). By injecting Urgent Genius into fashion, MITN have made our philosophy a lifestyle. Oh, and each design is available for just twenty-four hours, meaning that their customers also have to act in an Urgent Genius way, too.

Old Spice Response

 Old Spice

 Wieden + Kennedy

 USA

2010 – 2011

'The man your man could smell like' truly caught the imagination of the world. With 186 personalized videos, created in just two-and-a-half days and sent to influential tweeters, it's a casebook example of utilizing an Urgent Genius mindset. It was the first time an advertising campaign had harnessed the power of personalized film responses. The quality of the writing and the targeting of influencers made it incredibly effective.

1.8 billion recorded impressions for the brand across social media.

OldSpice

⁺⚏ Follow   ☰ Lists ▼   ⚙ ▼

Well @mindtakerr. First off your name is intimidating and I like that.
http://www.youtube.com/watch?v=WdKAXHWOkPc
13 minutes ago via web

Levi Hunter writes on fb Is it Old Spice that gives you magical powers or were you born awesome?
http://www.youtube.com/watch?v=WFt78fd70Xw
24 minutes ago via web

My life would be complete if I could get the old spice guy to reply to me (via @mickey_gousset)
http://www.youtube.com/watch?v=oO760tUHfGQ
31 minutes ago via web

BECOME ONE OF THE FRESHEST SMELLING PLACES ON EARTH.

Old Spice

'Experiment often. Fail fast. Learn quicker.'

8. Urgent Genius experiments

We've spent the last seven chapters looking at the very best examples of Urgent Genius from around the globe. We've illustrated the principles behind the mindset, and sure, they may have changed a few dozen times by the time you read this as that's the nature of taking a snapshot of a fast-moving, googly-eyed creature.

It's clear that there are creative agencies and individuals out there who are proving that it's possible to produce brilliance at speed. They employ hybrid thinkers who are keen to do it all – write, art direct, design, direct and edit. Basically, a bunch of control freaks, you're thinking? Actually, the spirit is more collaborative. It's all about timing. Sure, it's nice to bring in an expert editor, but if there's no time, then there are several people who count editing as one of their supplementary skills.

We like the way Robert Wong, creative director of Google's Creative Lab, describes what we think is the ideal Urgent Genius team:

'The Creative Lab employs fifty people from a range of disciplines – design, writing, coding – but all of them are united by their, um, "Googlyness,"…smart and multi-talented but also ambitious, humble and altruistic, but also with a sense of scale, like you feel like you can impact a lot of people with your work.'

At Google, they've certainly adopted the 'Think. Make. Launch.' It's all about getting out there and making things happen. We spend ages thinking about stuff too. A bit of planning makes our actions seem more spontaneous, actually. We also do a lot of thinking after the fact – like when you have loads of results and you need to figure out what worked and what didn't and why. And sometimes a bit of over-thinking happens because there's not always a clear indication, as a result of a little thing called luck that kicks in from time to time. If you're lucky, that is.

Tom Kelly, in his book *The Ten Faces of Innovation* has a different name for the

Urgent Genius that Google populate their lab with: 'The Experimenter prototypes new ideas continuously, learning by a process of enlightened trial and error. The Experimenter takes calculated risks to achieve success through a state of experimentation as implementation.'

Urgent Genius Weekender

Okay, Mr Wong and Mr Kelly, we've heard you. Now, it's time to find some of those people and start doing this stuff. So at the start of 2010, we were desperate to get our experimental genius on. We'd done our homework. We'd gathered various examples of Urgent Genius in action for a few months and incorporated the thinking into a few live projects. We were also populating the UrgentGenius.com blog every week with the latest in newsjacking and real-time awesomeness. Then we found out that we'd been invited to speak at the South By Southwest (SXSW) interactive festival 2011, in Austin, Texas.

It was action time. We needed to find our version of Googlyness. After a bit of phone banter between London and Singapore, we were a bit keen as we started to sort out our plan for global domination. Settle down, we thought. Maybe we should focus on a global competition. A few weeks later, we challenged the creative industry to see if they were up for embracing their inner Urgent Genius-ness. From our experience, creative types are super keen to break free from the constraints of the everyday client brief. You don't even have to beg them as they willingly put their reputations on the line to get their meme-making/culture-surfing/newsjacking/trend-riding Genius on for a weekend.

On 18 February 2011, we challenged teams from around the world to show us what a bit of time pressure and free pizza and beer could create in

our first ever Urgent Genius Weekender. Forty-eight hours to concept and create topical social ideas with the aim to see how many views, likes and interactions they could earn. We had over 100 team sign-ups from across the globe.

Of those teams, most of the American teams (Jon's people) 'wussed out' because of a minor scheduling oversight. The following Monday was a public holiday in the United States, so they dropped out like flies. Despite that, twenty-five teams got stuck in and created content in the forty-eight hours between 7 p.m. on Friday 18 February and 7 p.m. on Sunday 20 February. Teams from the UK, Singapore, Australia, South Africa and the United States (the hardcore teams) were pumped and ready to create. They

'There will be certain points of time when everything collides together and reaches critical mass around a new concept or a new thing that ends up being hugely relevant to a high percentage of people or businesses. But it's really really hard to predict those. I don't believe anyone can.'

Marc Andreessen, entrepreneur and co-founder of Netscape

were a mixture of individuals and agencies. They came from different backgrounds: film-production houses, global ad agencies, design collectives, social-media boutiques, digital shops and education establishments. Fallon UK, BBDO Singapore, iris worldwide, Ogilvy Sydney, Saatchi & Saatchi Cape Town, Modea, Albion, Bigballs Films, Salt TV, Lethal, FLNM, and Miami Ad School were just some of the names on the list.

We lined up an impressive panel of judges from ad agencies like Wieden+Kennedy, Droga5 and Crispin Porter+Bogusky. These included Luke Sullivan, former CD of GSDM in Austin and author of the advertising copywriter's bible *Hey, Whipple, Squeeze This*, Gavin Gordon-Rogers, LBi Edinburgh and Dave Bedwood and Sam Ball from London hot-shop Lean Mean Fighting Machine. And to balance things out, we even got Matt Diffee, a *New Yorker* cartoonist, to approach everything from a totally left-field standpoint. To keep the focus on shareability and help with seeding, we even roped in viral marketing folks Chris Quigley and Matt Golding from Rubber Republic.

As a guide for the participants and the judges, we said that the responses would be evaluated in the following way:

Is it Urgent?

How swiftly did the idea hit?
Did it make the most of the opportunity?
Did it catch fire instantly or was it a slow burner?

Is it Genius?

How strong is the idea?
How good is the craft?
Is it entertaining or useful?
Does it allow participation?
Does it give the user something of real value?

We also knew that seeding would be crucial after the initial concepting period. So we considered the size of each team's network and assisted their seeding with tips on where to place the content as well as pushing the content through our Twitter, Facebook and BuzzFeed channels.

We released suggestions for global trending topics on Thursday 17 February to kick-start the teams' thinking. We picked Dead Island, the gore-filled Zombie game with the mesmerizing trailer as our global trending topic. From Thursday to Saturday it was fluctuating between number nine and six on the top-ten trends list on Twitter. Then on Friday night/Saturday morning, Radiohead's Thom Yorke's seriously strange/out-of-control dancing around in the new 'Lotus Flower' video took the trends list by storm. Many teams responded to it within hours with various other mash-ups being released over the following two days.

Speed was crucial to the success of the most popular Thom mash-up. 'Thom Whips His Hair' accompanied by Willow Smith's hit 'Whip My Hair' was the quickest response by the Miami Ad School guys in the iris London office. It made its way onto the dailyfill.com, Perez Hilton said he liked it more than the original and it garnered more than 120,000 views without any real seeding.

Bigballs, the London-based production company, produced their Chase & Status mash-up within half an hour. But instead of releasing it, they thought they had to wait until the end of the forty-eight-hour period. If it had been released before 'Thom Whips His Hair' it may well have done better, but we'll never know. The Bigballs crew also created deleted scenes that featured a body double doing an excellent pastiche of Thom's dance moves. 'Never' saw Justin Bieber getting shot by Thom. There were various re-edits to alternative tunes with a couple of notable drum 'n' bass tunes and a Soulja Boy dub-step number. Another London effort saw a toy shop website advertising their very own 'Flailing-arms Thom'. 'Choreographer' featured a convincing performance that fooled many viewers (see page 198). Our fake choreographer waxed lyrical about how every move in the Radiohead video had been meticulously planned. The various Urgent Genius Thom re-cuts are among the most popular of the online incarnations that have created another internet meme. Three of the Urgent Genius creations made it into *Rolling Stone* magazine's top ten round-up of the Radiohead meme.

The main trending topic Dead Island produced gaming gloves, postcards from Dead Island, various other video mash-ups and zombie Tumblrs. The '*Shaun of the Dead* Island' by Dan Bull (see page 194) was put on the actual game publisher's blog, an amazing endorsement. Simon Pegg tweeted that it is 'the greatest trailer ever' for *Shaun of the Dead*, and Edgar Wright, the film's director, also wrote a piece on his blog.

Dan used a combination of Twitter, Facebook and YouTube, along with a more traditional approach: 'In terms of seeding, besides social media, I contacted individual journalists directly. That's how I got the news coverage. My angle was, "What if a Dead Island movie was made by the *Shaun of the Dead* guys"; two stories for the price of one, which I guess means a journo is twice as likely to be interested.' He rode the trending wave by tapping into one community while engaging another even more fanatical group. It garnered press coverage from *Metro*, *The Escapist* magazine and GameRant.com, and generated over 120,000 views. Dan was chuffed and he had this to say about the Urgent Genius Weekender:

'Thanks for the inspiration and incentive to do this, as otherwise I would have spent my weekend eating Doritos and watching *Star Trek*.' Dan Bull

The then-Italian prime minister Silvio Berlusconi hit the headlines over the Urgent Genus Weekender with the announcement of the date of his trial for allegedly paying for sex with an underage prostitute. 'Bunga or Bust' (see page 199) mashes up the Italian PM with 'Hot or Not' (Bunga Bunga being the name of his infamous sex parties). Berl's Big Perv (see page 200) allows you to chuck a few thousand Euros at lines of stripping girls Space Invader-style. A song called 'Bunga Bunga-low' (see page 201) asks 'How low will you go?' with Colonel Gaddafi on the mic. And a few smart infographics showed Berlusconi's prowess in bed.

In response to the spreading political unrest across the Middle East and North Africa, faceprotest.com allowed you to upload your own message on a placard and join the virtual protest online.

A few people asked us what was the point?

Well, it was the first of many UG experiments. There were failures and successes. And that was the point. We (everyone who entered the competition) got off our back sides and created for the love of it. We enjoyed it despite many of us only having a couple of hours' sleep during the weekend.

But on a more serious note, it questioned the structures and processes of both client organizations and creative agencies. Why is it that many agencies are still structured in exactly the same way as Sterling Cooper Draper Pryce of *Mad Men*? The traditional ad-agency creative department as we know it is dead. The agency of today, to be fit for the future, has to embrace proactivity. The old internal approval and production processes have to be parked. They're

too slow. There should be a new 'Go until I say stop' client approval process if you want to harness the power of real-time marketing.

'The search for the future is an exercise in edge finding. We don't know what we are looking for…We are working by instinct, by intuition…To find the innovation that returns lots and lots of value, we will have to try many things that return next to nothing. It's the nature of the hunt.'

Grant McCracken, *Culturematic*

Too often in our day-to-day lives we get caught up in the red tape of global organizations. The Weekender freed our creativity and encouraged us to take the plunge. We thank every one who took part – the enthusiasm and output was inspiring. Here are some responses from a few of those involved:

'This was a great first attempt into discovering whether brands can hijack topical events…Radiohead and Dead Island proved that they can get more traction and buzz…but there's still a big question mark on whether a brand can succeed riding a non-related buzz-worthy news story.' Jonathan Rosen/ Ryan O'Hara/Mary Crosse, Lucky Branded Entertainment, New York City

'Urgent Genius highlights the potential for how brands can become culture-friendly through positive contribution rather than interruption, and also have a much closer, multi-faceted and continual dialogue with people. This needs to be one piece of the puzzle of marketing communication of the next decade. Great competition.' Adam Springfeldt, Creative Director, Acne, Stockholm

'What's so exciting about Urgent Genius is that it asks you to make comedy about the world at large… and encourages completely different production techniques, giving you a direct line into audiences you wouldn't normally get.'

Will Saunders, Executive Producer, BBC Comedy

Urgent Genius Weekender 2

In 2012, we followed up with the second Weekender and signed up students at colleges across the UK and Singapore, alongside a few of the teams who entered the original Weekender.

It was an awesome experience seeing the next generation of creatives grappling with the Urgent Genius principles. The trending topics for the second Weekender unfortunately proved to be less spectacular than the first. The hot topics ranged from Justin Bieber turning eighteen to the *Despicable Me 2* trailer launching and the *Guardian*'s 'Three Little Pigs' television ad breaking in the UK.

A student team named DipShit London won the competition with their human version of the trailer for animated film *Despicable Me 2* (see page 203). It racked up the most views (250,000 in the week, it now has 750,000+) The effort the guys put in with their costumes really brought the piece to life. *Despicable Me* fans took a bit of a dislike to their homage but the views keep racking up. It demonstrates that you can generate a response if you understand how to tap into a passionate, connected fan base.

This is something the victor from our first competition understands only too well. Dan Bull has built up an engaged fan base via his razor-sharp YouTube rap videos and he demonstrated his lyrical credentials with a crowd-sourced film and track for our competition (see page 204). He managed to get hundreds of his fans to each hold up (and send in) a line of his rant against the British Polyphonic Industry. He then edited the various images into a video for his track. The film generated over 100,000 views in the first week alone – it was a really impressive crowd-sourced effort. The third highlight of the second Weekender was a rehash of the *Guardian*'s 'Three Little Pigs' television ad (see page 205). In Joe 'Jester' Jacobs' remix the ad is reworked for the UK's biggest tabloid newspaper the *Sun*.

Bumblecart, UK,
March 2011

But our Urgent Genius Weekender experiments weren't the first examples of iris folk getting involved in topical mash-ups. Andy Pilkington, iris London's Head of Moving Image, had tried a little experiment of his own (see page 206). The England football team, and

more specifically goalkeeper Robert Green, had a disastrous World Cup match against the United States (a game Jon holds as dear to him as Grant does England's one-and-only World Cup triumph in 1966). It resulted in a 1-1 draw, with the American goal owing to an almighty gaffe by Green. After watching the game, Andy decided to rewrite history in England's favour. An instant audience of embittered English football fans turned the clip viral, and the view count skyrocketed to over 500,000 in a matter of days. We spoke to the football-mad creator of the meme – a.k.a. Bumblecart – to find out more.

How soon after the match did you create it?

'The game was on Saturday and I put the video together the following Monday.'

Have you previously produced a mash-up that's generated massive views?

'I've played around with film footage plenty of times before, but only for a bit of a giggle. As I'd started to get a few thousand views for virtually no work or idea, I started to wonder how many hits I could get for a quick turnaround edit, and when I had the idea I knew it had legs, but I was completely shocked when it started to take off so quickly. The crazy thing is that 95 per cent of the hits the video has were in the first two weeks it went live.'

How did you create the video and what technical tricks helped you to pull it off so flawlessly?

'The real trick is in the footage itself – in that Robert Green's body movement allowed me to paint out and re-impose the ball in places that looked quite natural. In relation to my technical capability, it's a real hatchet job and there are a lot of glitches and bits and pieces I could have fixed, but for me this was about doing the minimum amount required to make the gag work. It's actually quite nice to leave those little clues in there for people to review and watch again to see how I did it!'

Then after it was made…how did you seed it? Or did you seed it at all?

'All I did was tag a video response to an upload of the real footage, and linked it on my Facebook page.'

Where did you get the voice-over, 'a fantastic save by Rob Green'…(so very poignant!)?

'It's just a sound bite from later in the game where poor old Rob does make a decent save! All these kind of videos are really about trawling through your footage and knowing what you have to work with.'

Did you track the progress as the number of views grew?

'I closely monitored how things progressed so I could retain the data for any viral work I did in my day job. That was kind of the point for me.

I didn't want to spend any money or effort on this…it needed to be the idea that did the work. The first couple of days were slower, with a few thousand hits, but as I searched Google I found literally hundreds of links and mentions around the world on every kind of site, and from that point the hits went through the roof. Within a few days it was on the BBC, in the national newspapers and even on ITV's breakfast show. I actually choked on some cornflakes when it came on one morning. By the end of the first week, it was at 500,000 hits, but the TV show took it up to about 700,000 almost overnight. I think my favourite stat was that it was rated three places higher than Carlsberg's official World Cup TV ad on Unruly's Viral Video Chart. I felt smug…two hours on After Effects versus a couple of million quid. Very smug.'

Now, if you're reading this chronologically, you've just had several pages of words, so it's time to get to the fun part. This is the doing bit that we live for. Here you go – loads of pictures of all these Urgent Genius experiments that may, if we're lucky, inspire you to join our next Weekender.

8

URGENT GENIUS WEEKENDER

18TH, 19TH & 20TH FEBRUARY 2011

With our talk confirmed at SXSW 2011, we wanted to put our theory to the test. We put out the call for creative teams to go head-to-head to create content over a forty-eight-hour weekender with the simple aim of trying to generate the most views and shares by vibing off a top-ten trending topic. We were amazed at the response and even more delighted by some of the entries. In total, 150 pieces of content were created by twenty-five teams around the globe. Over the next few pages we'll share some of the highlights from the Urgent Genius Weekender.

'If we relate this project back to brands, Dead Island and Radiohead certainly got additional PR for their brands this weekend because of Urgent Genius!'

Dave Bedwood, Creative Partner, Lean Mean Fighting Machine

The Dead Island trailer was one of the top Twitter trending topics as The Urgent Genius Weekender started. It told the story of a family visiting the resort running in slow motion and in reverse. The haunting soundtrack pushed the clip into the most-viewed charts. Dan Bull, our winner of the first Weekender, came up with the inspired idea of '*Shaun of the Dead* Island'. He reversed scenes from the comedy zombie flick and recut them to the Dead Island track. The result resonated with fans of both the game and the film. And Simon Pegg, the lead actor, and Edgar Wright, the Director, both tweeted about it, resulting in 120,000 views for Dan within a week. Not bad for a guy who was going to stay in and watch *Star Trek*.

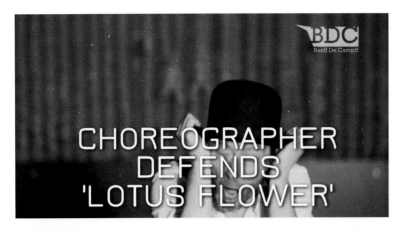

Left: **Choreographer Defends 'Lotus Flower' by iris London and Banff De Campff**

The performance by Kevin McGlade was so convincing that people really thought that he was the choreographer. The clip featured an impassioned defence of Yorke's pretentious prancing. When the interviewer questioned the choreographer he replied with the classic line: 'What's a dance background? A certificate that says you can express yourself?'

Opposite: **Deleted Scenes by Bigballs**

The Bigballs effort featured a look-a-like pulling various absurd dance moves. The team used a green screen to comp the 'deleted' scenes into the original. It took them the full forty-eight hours to complete the piece but it was definitely one of the funniest Radiohead responses.

Below: Three of the Radiohead mash-ups from The Weekender made the Rolling Stones round-up of the top ten Radiohead memes.

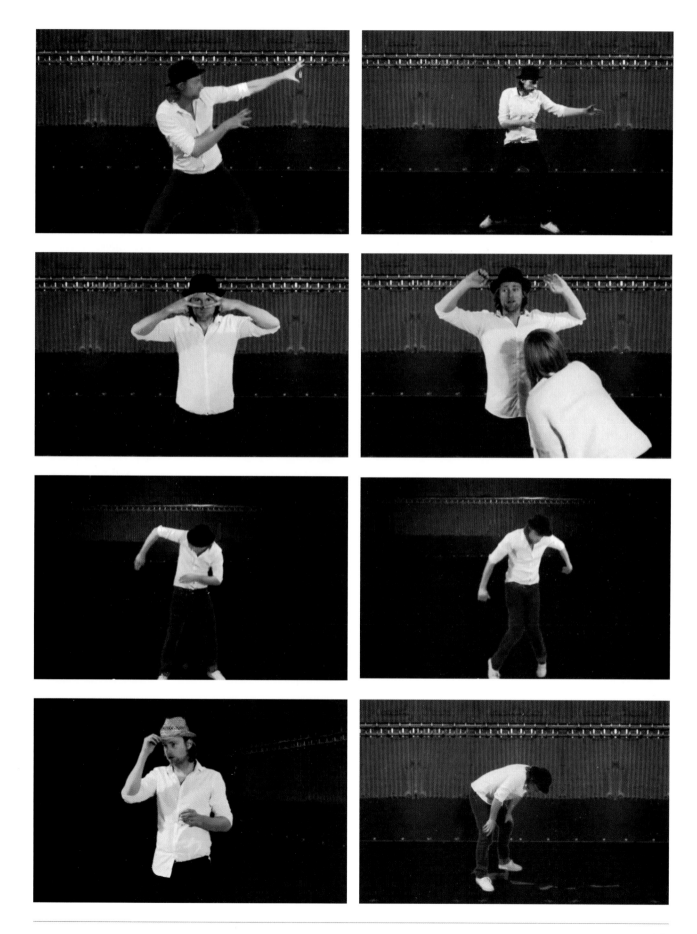

BUNGA
BUNGA
PARTIES

The Silvio Berlusconi scandal was a hot topic. His infamous 'Bunga Bunga' parties where various girls were invited to party and were supposedly paid for their services generated massive social buzz. One girl in particular, known as 'Ruby', was only seventeen at the alleged time she attended one of Silvio's parties. A number of our teams took up the challenge and created satirical takes on the then-Italian PM's antics.

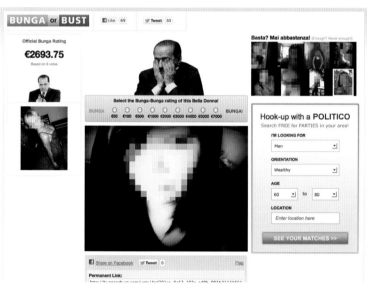

Left: **Bunga or Bust by iris London**

Ashley Taylor, Tim Holden and Bill Adcock of iris London created a Hot or Not mash-up called Bunga or Bust. The familiar Hot or Not interface was re-skinned with how much Silvio would be willing to pay for a night with the young lady featured. Although politically incorrect, it proved to be a perfect fit with the young male market as the site was bought by a 'lads mag' in the UK.

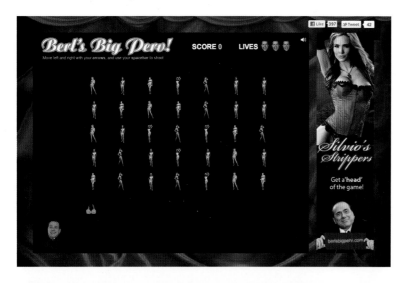

Left: **Big Berl's Perv**

Two separate teams in Singapore created two microsites. The first, Big Berl's Perv cast Silvio as a money-chucking pervert throwing cash at lines of stripping girls. It was a naughty take on the classic video game Space Invaders.

Right: **Bunga Bunga-low**

Bunga Bunga-low was a song and a microsite where you had to enter your age to get in. The catch being that no matter how low you went, you'd never be young enough.

Berlusconi's BUNGA BUNGA-LOW

Welcome to my Bunga Bungalow all you bellisimo beauties. You're about to experience the time of your life. But before you get all excited and giggly, tell me about yourself. I want to make sure that you're ripe for some bunga bunga. — *Silvio*

Name  Age   Come Inside

Bunga Bunga-low by Berlusconi featuring the Colonel on Rogue State recordings - full release 6th April

URGENT GENIUS 2 WEEKENDER

3RD, 4TH & 5TH MARCH 2012

Our second Urgent Genius Weekender took place in March 2012. This time we put a focus on students and invited colleges to get involved, as well as some of the contributors from the original competition. In London, Jon led a gathering of creatives and tech-heads to work together over the forty-eight hours. In Singapore, Grant briefed Singapore students and groups of iris folks in Asia. The trending topics weren't as sensational as the weekender in 2011 but the competitors still managed to generate content that attracted eyeballs.

Forty-eight hours to find the next generation of Urgent Geniuses.

Above: **Despicable Me 2 by London College of Communication's team, Dipshit**

The Weekender began on the same day as the trailer for *Despicable Me 2* was the talk of the internet. London College of Communication's team Dipshit responded with this painstaking human recreation of it. The urgency of its posting saw it quickly rack up a huge amount of views in a short space of time. It even got mentions in a few newspapers after its release. Views after seven days: 206,000.

Overleaf: **Bye Bye BPI by Dan Bull**

Dan Bull released his song 'Bye Bye BPI' as a response to ongoing discussions involving internet piracy. To garner more attention, he approached his fans directly and asked them to take part in his own video by picturing themselves holding a sheet of lyrics from the song and a musical instrument. The song proved a huge viral hit, not only being retweeted by Stephen Fry but also getting posted on The Pirate Bay homepage.

Tits, pedos,football

Above: **Three Little Pigs for the *Sun* by iris London**

This response to a hugely popular *Guardian* advert featuring a modern interpretation of the Three Little Pigs story, from iris London's Joe Jacobs and Tom Prendergast, showed the *Sun*'s understanding of the same story. This was released a mere two days after the original ad, while it was still fresh in people's minds.

'Two million quid vs two hours on After Effects to change history.'
Bumblecart

www.urgentgenius.com

www.boobstagram.com

www.boobstagram.com

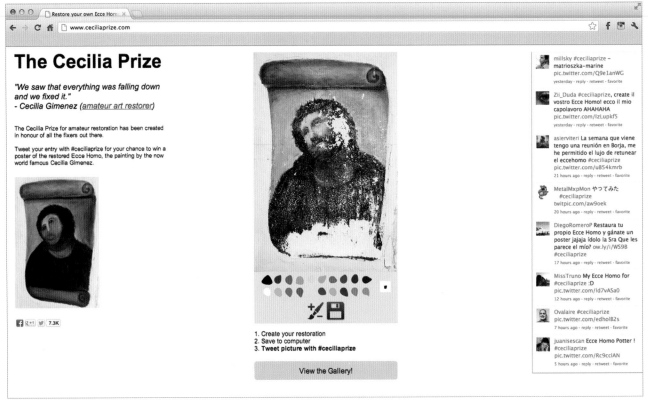

From big boobs to a bit of a booboo
Top: **Boobstagram** *Bottom:* **The Cecilia Prize**

Final thoughts

Okay, so how do we summarize a book of case studies? With more case studies. Ones that just popped up on our radar as this little book was going to print. Ones that represent the future. So we've got a few more case studies in us before we kick back with an Urgent Genius craft beer with topical labels that change every day Tim Horton style (see page 109). So no celebrations just yet…

These two interactive platforms are easily replicable. They were all launched quickly. Timing and speed were everything. Both were really funny and got people to do something quite irreverent. One involved boobs. Now, if we had a third one that allowed you to do something cute with kittens, we'd have the future laid out for you totally.

Cecelia Prize

The world's media showcased the talents of Cecilia Giménez, an amateur art restorer in Spain. She noticed that the painting *Ecce Homo* by the renowned artist Elías García Martíne was in need of some love and a makeover. Her 'abstraction' was truly awful, but so funny.

BBH rode the wave and have created this sweet little site: www.ceciliaprize.com It allowed you to restore the masterpiece or create one of your own and tweet it to the gallery. The best ones were awarded 'The Cecilia Prize'.

Boobstagram

It goes without saying that a photograph of a pair of boobs is among the most valuable currency on the internet. Combine that with the hipster powerhouse that is Instagram and what do you have? To raise awareness of Breast Cancer month, Boobstagram was created to serve an aesthetically pleasing resource for the cause. But what began as a simple exercise in planned spontaneity has now become essentially an Urgent Genius topical platform. More and more women have been using their boob pictures to champion other topical causes such as gay rights, forthcoming elections and the prostate and testicular cancer charity-sponsored Movember (see page 132). Hats off to the two breast-loving Frenchmen who saw the potential of sourcing existing Instagram images and using them as a charitable call to action.

The 13 UG challenges

Everyone loves lists. That's a great way to end a book, don't you think? Well, we've learned a lot since we first locked down the structure of this beast of a book. Here are a few pointers that you can take with you to further focus your Urgent Genius experiments in the future:

1. Live and breathe culture

Wait for it. Here comes an über-obvious one, but we've got to mention it because ad people can get caught up in, well, ads: Be a student of culture. Be obsessive in following your passions and interests. Don't just be an ad geek. Dive deep into films, music, books, tech, gadgets, sport and so on, to give you a rounder knowledge that will inform your work.

2. Feel overwhelmed by information

Feel overwhelmed by all the info overload online and the scattered attention spans of yourself, your clients and their customers.

3. Categorize culture into little content pots

Make sense of the mess for yourself. Put it into folders or pots or networks or whatever you want to call them. Use fancy dashboards that do it for you. You will need these to gain insights to convince clients that a slow-growing trend is gaining attention and therefore you need to be the first to capitalize on it when the time is right.

4. Do a deep dive into the data

Spot patterns in what's happening online and how brands/individuals/channels are using newsjacking to climb to the top of Mount Google.

5. Find a way to visualize the data in a mind-blowing way and personalize it for each client

This is important because you must bring some method to the madness. Clients need eventually to do their own listening/monitoring and be so in tune with it that they are structuring their organization around it.

6. Build your newsroom

You've got your networks and your data viz in place. Now you must embed it into the fabric of your agency.

7. Build a hybrid army

Through associations with universities/colleges and coding-course grads, you must build an army of people who are on standby for when a brief comes in. These must be hybrid thinkers. They must want to do it all. Write. Art direct. Produce. Learn to code. You must organize hack days to test them and create your A-Team around various topics. If you have a sport client, you need to have a team that lives and breathes sport. Your creative department will not be able to handle this task. It requires full attention.

8. Find content partner allies

Realize that you won't be able to do everything yourself. You need to have content partnerships in place at the very beginning. Broker deals with content makers who will be willing to go in with an experiment with you. Urgent Genius needs professionals as much as it needs young and hungry hybrids.

9. Find the right opportunity

The brief from the client is the most important aspect. What does the client want from an Urgent Genius experiment? What are their creative goals? Sales goals? Risk tolerance? What is their approvals process?

10. Prepare for battle

Get your army ready by building structures in which they can fight when it all kicks off. Several hack days will help you create these interactive platforms that are rough and ready to skin and rework for whatever's trending.

11. Lay down the ground rules

If a client is up for the challenge, he/she must be willing to play by the UG rules. You must create stuff in advance that you know will have high energy and cultural relevance – Olympics, national elections, The Oscars, holidays, etc.

12. Together we ride

This is where it's crucial to have the total trust of the client. You've shown them the templates – now they must trust you to skin them for the appropriate trigger and launch them with their blessing because they've already had the skin approved by legal.

13. Analyse how you've done

We're developing the Urgent Genius Performance Index, which rates what you've done and how it performed online. You need to find or make something similar to help you learn from your mistakes. Even if that mistake is mentioning the Index before it's finished in the hope that it will be ready when this book hits the shelves.

How to be an Urgent Genius

Along the way, we've learned many tricks, tips and trade secrets about how to get brilliant work done quickly. Problem is, these change every day, but over the last few years we've definitely gathered some thoughts that guide our quest to help clients be more relevant and timely. Since we turned in the final draft of this book to the publisher, we've probably added several new ones to this list on urgentgenius.com and removed a few of the ones that – with hindsight – made absolutely no sense. So use the QR codes to check out all the up-to-the-minute content on the website and feel free to add a few thoughts of your own.

Give it the death-threat test

The guy who inspired us to create Urgent Genius got death threats for his interactive site that pokes fun at the racist British National Party in the UK. Is your idea so shareable and viral you could add a few 'death threats' to the CV?

Make it a Trenta

Urgent Genius asks you to try things on that seem plain wrong. Like Starbucks' new size, Trenta. Studies proved that this cup housed more liquid than the average stomach could hold. It didn't catch on, even in the most obese regions of the United States, but it made headlines. Next time, go for an idea that's super huge but do-able.

Learn the language

The language of the internet is code. We must all learn the basics of programming at the very least. Would you move to a foreign country and refuse to speak the language? By the time you read this, Jon will have spoken at SXSW 2013 about The London Teenage Code Riot (Google it). It's about his efforts to teach teenagers to code. Not just any teens. Some that were involved in the London riots of 2011. Start with a one-day course from the lovely folks at Decoded.co or a similar tech school near you.

One-leg meetings

You need to be out there making stuff, not meeting to talk about making stuff. So if you all meet standing up on one leg and the meeting only lasts as long as it takes for the last person to fall, you'll be quick and concise, so you can get back to creating genius.

Read a thousand books a year

The 'Get A Free Sample' feature on Amazon's Kindle is brilliant. As a professional Urgent Genius dabbler and tinkerer, you need to poke sticks at your brain to activate it and teach it a little bit about a lot of stuff.

Cut off your life support

We know this may seem impossible as a digital native, but switching off from the internet for an hour a day during work hours may help you discover something new. We also suggest trying to go totally analogue (except for digital books, of course) after 10 p.m., but that may seem heretical to you. That's fine. Try it.

Electrocute yourself

Dabble with the starter electronics kit that is Arduino. Build a bridge between the digital and physical by tinkering; hack into stuff and repurpose it. We love ideas like Beeri, which newsjacked Apple's voice assistant Siri, enabling a voice command to activate an Arduino-powered remote control truck to pour someone a beer. We all need to be dabbling in this sort of thing to expand our minds.

Wreck the reception area

Urgent Genius is all about gaining the client's trust. And it's about taking risks and making a good first impression with prospective clients who have an appetite for such risk. Advertising legend Steve Henry told us about how agency KesselsKramer turned their reception into a strip club by asking everyone who entered the agency to take a Polaroid picture of their nipple. Brilliant. How can you make sure your client's first impressions aren't your first-thought safe ideas? Maybe by not showing them and throwing a brick through the window? Maybe throw that brick around reception if you think it will help.

Stalk people – with permission

Okay, so you're going to need to know a little about everything to be a proper Urgent Genius. So it's time to be bold. Ask people if you can

shadow them for a day. Tell them you won't say a word. Just go with them to their meetings, hold a graffiti artist's spray cans or follow them down the fireman's pole and into the hook and ladder to save that kitten. Maybe forget the last one. Make sure your stalking is totally work-related and not just a childhood dream.

Skype the world

We give Urgent Genius presentations all around the world. We learn so much about other creative cultures and other ways of working. Why not have brainstorms with folks all around the world – just to learn a new way of doing things. Time zones can be tricky but it's worth having regular Skype sessions with people you admire and can learn from. Even über-busy people. Try them. It doesn't take much to turn on a webcam for fifteen minutes.

Boggle your mind, then add beer

You need to be very close and comfortable with all your co-collaborators – especially on a high-pressure Urgent Genius weekend. There's no better way to build a bit of rivalry and flex different sides of the brain than with a nice few rounds of the word-scramble game Boggle. Add beer for more fun.

Master the memes

Every week, someone on your team should study the week's memes and present what's happening and why, and how this relates to current clients.

Urgent Genius is...

1. Staying up to date and feeling outdated in the same breath.

2. Futuristic like teleportation, but sometimes feels more like a Segway tour.

3. About being time-poor and information-rich and loving it.

4. Putting systems in place to deal with the onslaught.

5. Never watching anything passively ever again.

6. Driving your wife crazy. Just one last Tweet…

7. Reading everything. Not skimming.

8. Writing in short sentences.

9. Trying to keep your manifestos short. And failing.

10. Maybe it's more about bullet points?

   - They're more digestible.
   - They're more URGENT.
   - Especially in ALL-CAPS.

11. Finding gadgets that understand you. That know you…

…That become you. Like Flipboard and Zite.

12. Spending too much time on Kickstarter and Reddit.

13. Piggybacking. It's re-purposing. It's trying to influence culture.

14. Newsjacking those who newsjacked you.

15. Finding a new word for newsjacking.

16. Culture-surfing. No, it's not. You tell us what it is: _____

17. Tapping into the wisdom of the crowd but not counting on them to deliver.

18. Asking the experts. But not asking for too much.

19. Just being switched on. It's about helping clients be brave.

20. Wanting to point an HD camera at something and then thinking it through afterwards.

21. Planning things so meticulously that it looks like you just went out and shot something on a whim.

22. Going totally analogue before your brain explodes.

23. Forgetting platforms and enjoying the smell of a print ad. A topical one of course.

24. Learning to code. Then teaching teens to do it. It's building your army. Your mobile army.

25. Not having an office. Or if you have to, then having a trapeze in reception. And not explaining why. Ever.

26. It's trading your Moleskin for Post-it notes and Instagram. For a week.

27. It's wishing you were Ze Frank. Or at least wishing that your little movement started with a video called 'How to Dance Properly'.

28. Writing manifestos like this. No, it's making a manifesto e-book. One where each page is a surprise.

29. Channelling Benrik and hoping that your next book will change lives.

30. Committing to doing. Thinking. Making. Launching.

31. Writing a book with a seven-month lead time.

32. Not worrying about it being outdated, but seeing it as a glimpse of something that's too fast to publish.

33. Like taking a Polaroid of a cheetah.

34. Probably none of this now because times are a-changing.

35. Refusing to look at the keyboard for twenty minutes and hoping that you've written something special and/or coherent as you keep your hands moving. Sometimes it's Accidental Genius.

Go forth and make

Every ad campaign has one so, shouldn't a book on advertising? Well, this call to action changes every day, so we'll keep it general. This is what Urgent Genius looks like:

We come into your organization. We show you a few shiny tools we're developing to add a bit of method to the madness.

We interview your team. We find out who does what. More importantly, we find out what people are passionate about. We analyse your clients. We consider which ones have a higher Urgent Genius IQ. We run their records through the Urgent Genius Opportunity Index (which we've been dreaming about since 2011 and will hopefully be operational by the time you're reading this). It highlights the opportunities in the cultural calendar that you should be interested in. The ones that fit your brand like a fingerless glove. Smell the glove. Nice isn't it? Yes, we will try to get 'Christopher *Spinal Tap* Guest' involved with your brand. And if we're really genius, we'll get him to waive his substantial appearance fee.

What started out as marketing for the attention-deficient (ourselves) is now a mini-movement to turn brands into relevant creatures.

David Meerman Scott's e-book *Newsjacking* is worth reading. It talks about using newsjacking as a PR tool to own the second paragraph. Our little movement is less a PR tool and more a philosophy on how to build armies of meme-makers and culture-jackers. We see our crew meshing perfectly with David's PR tool, making interactive tools in the time it takes to write a press release and climb all the way to the top of Google. And if we're really lucky, we may even get to create a physical object that's powered by real-time data. The future, for us, lies in people who can think and do. And we see great power in being able to create something physical that's digitally connected.

Here are five of the first efforts we stumbled upon a few years ago that inspired us to dabble in Arduino and physical computing. This was only the beginning, but we've run out of space and time to share with you all our favourite 'social objects', so you'll have to wander over to urgentgenius.com for more.

Digital meets physical

Enter the Internet of Things. It's smart technology gone wild. Red Bull Creation is the future. So is Maker Faire. The agency or individual that can infiltrate the consumer mindset with beautiful and useful digitally connected 'things' that are über-relevant to their current needs and interests will win. Context is king.

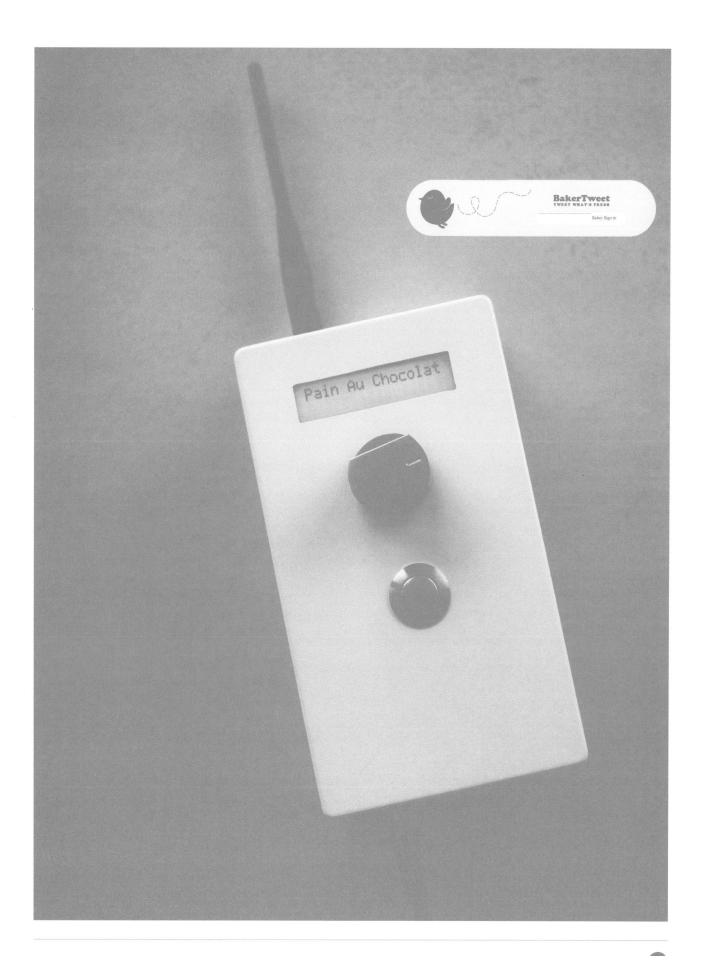

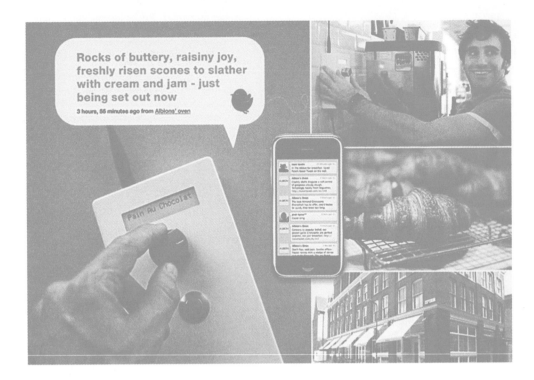

BakerTweet

London agency Poke has devised a way of letting fresh-bread lovers know the moment their local baker opens his oven door. BakerTweet uses a modified Arduino circuit board to trigger a tweet to hungry customers. It was launched at Albion Cafe in Shoreditch, London, where local office workers can pop out for a warm pastry the moment they hear from @AlbionsOven.

Change the Tune

Is there an acceptable way to protest at your work colleague's taste in music? Agency Republic created the Change the Tune poster that nudges the office's shared playlist on to the next track when a ball of scrunched-up paper is thrown at it. The poster hides a motion sensor wired to the music player via an Arduino nano.

Okay, for the next social object, we've moved back to the heart of the matter – using tech to stuff your pie hole. Or in this case, pizza hole.

Pizza fridge button

Could ordering pizza get any easier? Red Tomato, a pizza restaurant in Dubai has developed an intelligent fridge magnet that places your order with a single press.

The device remembers your customized order and sends it to the restaurant via your home hub. The button is designed with a flap – like a box lid – to save you accidentally ordering whenever you lean on the fridge door.

Plants that tweet when thirsty

So far, social objects have been very 'you' focused. What about the environment? Don't you care about it? Well, while you're working every hour God created, what are your plants thinking about? How you haven't watered them in weeks? Now, you can be selfish and considerate. To your plants at least.

We talk to our plants but never expected them to talk back to us. Botanicalls is an innovator of plant-to-human communications and has developed a system for plants to tell us when they need watering. The Botanicalls Kit comes with two probes that monitor soil moisture levels. When the plant needs watering, its owner receives a tweet generated by a built-in microcontroller.

TweetFuel

And while you're sorting out your approach to the environment, might you want to think about your declining health? You work too much, but that won't change. So let's look at the health of your Twitter account instead. Stinkdigital has created a novel way of measuring activity on Twitter accounts. They've attached a

Nike+ FuelBand to a small motor that rotates faster whenever there is an increase in follows and re-tweets. In case we need any further encouragement to tweet, the agency has created a smart time-line graphic to display our peaks and troughs of micro-blogging.

We hope you've enjoyed your lazy Sunday afternoon reading this book. It's now time to call up a few mates, find a space to create and just start experimenting. Oh, and then let us know about it at urgentgenius.com. And please do something mind-blowing with 3D printing as we've been watching this space with giddy anticipation. Final Urgent Genius challenge for you: if you can find a way to 3D print us some Krispy Kreme doughnuts, get your creation on Kickstarter, kick back and relax. Your work is done.

1 hour, 7 minutes ago from Albion's oven

REFERENCES

INTRODUCTION

Slap Nick Griffin, p7
Interview with Jon Plackett

Steve Jobs quote, p7
http://www.bigisthenewsmall.com/
2011/10/09/top-15-steve-jobs-quotes/

Paris Hilton quote, p7
http://www.mrselfdevelopment.com/
2010/01/9-success-lessons-from-
paris-hilton/

Lynx Britney Wedding, p8
http://www.nmauk.co.uk/nma/do/live/
breakingads?showBrowse=false&
creativeModel=1637
http://www.bbc.co.uk/news/
entertainment-arts-18076207
Email correspondence with BBH London

Ikea John Howard Chairs, p9
Email interview with Host

Veet Goodbye Bush, p10
Email interview with Steve Coll ECD

DPT Garage Doors, p11
Email interview with David Asmussen,
23 January 2012

Macy & Thompson quote, p12
http://blog.westinteractive.com/
2011/08/25/did-it-happen-or-not/

E. Schmidt quote, p13
http://techcrunch.com/2010/08/04/
schmidt-data/

YouTube quote, p13
http://www.youtube.com/watch?
v=sHPfc6wha5k

CHAPTER 1

David Meerman Scott quote, p16
Paraphrase of 'Power Rule' in *Real-Time
Marketing and PR*, John Wiley & Sons, 2010

Jarod Kintz quote, p18
http://www.goodreads.com/quotes/453989-
the-essence-of-courage-is-timing-take-me-
for-example/

2SickBastards, p18
Interview with Ben Aldis, 25 July 2011

SuperSocial, p19
Email interview with Max Rietbergen
SuperSocial, 2 August 2011

Scoopshot, p20
Email interview with Niko Ruokosuo and
Petri Rahja, 24 October 2011

Rohit Bhargava quote, p20
http://likeonomics.com/wp-content/uploads/
2012/05/Likeonomics_Ch8_Timing.pdf

Scott Adams quote, p21
http://www.goodreads.com/quotes/472168-
your-best-work-involves-timing-if-someone-
wrote-the-best

Nando's, p21
Interview with Ahmed Tilly, 10 July 2012

John Kotter quote, p22
http://www.fastcompany.com/1838047/your-
timing-sucks-and-its-killing-sales-3-ways-
get-it-right

Leonardo da Vinci quote, p23
http://www.brainyquote.com/quotes/
keywords/urgency

Synergy Chalkboards, p28
Email interview with Joe D'Allegro

PUMA Index, p30
viralblog.com 12 September 2009,
The D&AD Annual 2010, Taschen
Interview with Droga5 New York,
March 2012

Wikileaks…Butterfly Doesn't, p34
Newser, 16 December 2010,
Divanee, 20 December 2010,
Email interview with S. Amjad Hussain,
19 October 2011

Steve Jobs RIP
Email interview with Jonathan Mak

CHAPTER 2

Michael Logan quote, p40
Phone interview with Michael Logan from
NMA, 1 April 2011

Who Killed Summer, p42
Interview with Richard Welsh, Head
of Development at Bigballs, London,
15 April 2011

Tom Kelly quote, p42
http://compassioninpolitics.wordpress.
com/2010/07/26/quotes-from-tom-kelley-
on-innovation/

Longshot, p42
Interview with Sarah Rich, *Longshot* editorial
team, 17 April 2011

adidas 2010 World Cup, p44
Interview with Dan Brooks, Creative and
Director, 6 April 2010

SuperSwypers, p45
Digital Buzzblog, 1 November 2010,
Case study video
Email interview with Karlijn van der Berg,
Ice Mobile

Johann Wolfgang Von Goethe quote, p45
http://linguaspectrum.com/quotations/
by_author_english.php?quoteoftheday_
author=Johann%20Wolfgang%20von%
20Goethe

Ikea 365, p46
Email interview with Robin Stam,
Art Director, 22 April 2011

John Naisbitt quote, p46
http://www.finestquotes.com/author_quotes-
author-John+Naisbitt-page-0.htm

Next Media Animation, p47
Phone interview with Michael Logan from
NMA, 1 April 2011
Wired article 30 August 2010

Step Inside the Circuit, p58
Interview Ewan Topping, Diageo,
iris-worldwide.com

Hotel Casa Camper, p60
http://www.hotelcasacamper.tv/
Interview with Boolab

IKEA 365, p62
Skype interview with Remico Marinus Lemz,
January 2012

CHAPTER 3

Bas and Dan quote, p64
Email interview with Bas and Dan
of Wonderyears

Don't Hate on Kate, p66
Email Interview with Stika and Monorex, 2011

Mark Twain quote, p66
http://www.twainquotes.com/Discovery.html

KK Outlet plates, p67
Phone interview with Richard Walkers,
Creative Director, KK Outlet

Dutch Football Shirt, p68
Email interview with Bas and Dan
of Wonderyears

World Cup Octopuppy, p69
Email interview with Valerie Cheng,
30 January 2012

Seth Godin quote, p69
http://www.thinq.net/blog/bid/78929/
3-Small-Business-Tips-from-Seth-Godin-
s-Linchpin

Thriller Drinks, p70
Email interview, Mike Haliechuk from
Fucked Up, August 2011

Akas Ahmed quote, p70
http://www.adweek.com/news/advertising-
branding/fast-chat-ajaz-ahmeds-new-
book-139983

Re35, p71
Interview with Rogge and Pott, Hamburg

Heineken Super Social Christmas Tree, p82
iris-worldwide.com

McDonalds Shamrock Shake
Email interview with Brian Shembeda and
Avery Gross, Leo Burnett Chicago

CHAPTER 4

Anthony Ganjou quote, p88
Email interview with Anthony Ganjou,
CEO Curb Media, 1 June 2012

Sam Ball quote, p90
http://109.123.100.116/home/blog/
creative-social-where-digital-meets-real.html

Grey Mood Clock, p91
Email interview with Carl Jones, Grey Canada

Whopper Face, p91
Email interview with Angela Bassichetti,
6 September 2011

VW Winter Adjusted Offer, p92
Interview with Simon Higby, DDB Stockholm
http://www.vwskiteam.se/en/

BA Caribbean Live, p93
Email interview with Charlotte Bates at
Connected Pictures

Bacterial Billboard, p94
Email interview with Anthony Ganjou,
CEO Curb Media, 1 June 2012
http://news.sciencemag.org/
scienceinsider/2011/09/dont-call-it-viral-
marketing-the.html

Parking Douche, p95
Interview with Vladimir Shreyder,
7 July 2012

Life Scoreboard, p97
Interview with Droga5 New York

WWF Melting QR Codes, p101
Interview Tom Ormes April 2012

Heineken Star Player, p102
Andy Hood presentation at 2Screen 2011
https://vimeo.com/31423385
Email interview with Andy Hood

Last FM Festival, p103
Email interview with Rehab Studios,
October 2011
http://www.last.fm/group/Last.fm+Festival

CHAPTER 5

Movember quote, p112
http://uk.movember.com/about/

Movember, p114
Interview with Adam Garone, 27 July 2012

Susan F. Benjamin quote, p114
*Flash! How to Market Your Company in Today's
Instant World*, Adams Business, 2010

International Day for Dreamers, p118
Interview with Ozioma Egwuonwu,
23 July 2012

Patagonia's Cyber Monday, p121
http://www.patagonia.com/
email/11/112811.html
http://www.huffingtonpost.
com/2011/11/28/patagonia-common-
threads-initiative_n_1116901.html

National Cleavage Day, p122
Case study video from iris worldwide
http://www.huffingtonpost.
co.uk/2012/03/30/national-cleavage-day-
holly-willoughby-wins-best-breasts-with-
scarlett-johansson-and-beyonce-in-hot-
pursuit_n_1390409.html#s826700

National Day of Unplugging, p126
http://mashable.com/2012/03/22/national-
day-of-unplugging/

WWF Sweater Day, p128
http://www.adverblog.com/2012/02/01/
grannies-call-you-on-sweater-day/
http://strategyonline.ca/2012/02/02/
wwf-rallies-grannies-to-help-fight-climate-
change/
http://www.wwf.ca/takeaction/sweater_day/

The Good Times, p129
http://goodtimes.thechurchoflondon.com/

Rally to Restore Sanity and/or Fear, p130
http://www.buzzfeed.com/mjs538/the-100-
best-signs-at-the-rally-to-restore-sanity
http://www.guardian.co.uk/media/2010/
oct/31/rally-restore-sanity-jon-stewart-
washington
http://www.rallytorestoresanity.com/

CHAPTER 6

Nina quote, p136
Interview with Megan Wyatt,
15 September 2011

Henry David Thoreau quote, p137
http://www.brainyquote.com/quotes/
quotes/h/henrydavid108059.html

Paper Cranes for Japan, p138
Interview with Megan Wyatt,
15 September 2011
http://studentsrebuild.org/blog/1783/
action-alert-paper-cranes-japan.html

Drake quote, p139
http://m.vh1.com/news/article.
rbml?id=1685909

Chilean Miners, Oakley, p139
Oakley.com press room, 13 October 2010
CNBC.com, 13 October
Huffington Post, 13 October
The *Telegraph*, 8 October 2010

Bronx Zoo's Cobra, p141
Email interview with the cobra, 14 July 2011
Via PurpleList
Deanna Lawrence, 16 April 2011
http://nymag.com/daily/intel/2011/03/
dont_freak_out_but_a_poisonous.html

Mark Zuckerburg quote, p143
http://thoughtcatalog.com/2011/
unfortunately-the-internet-may-be-making-
us-dumber/

Daikon Crop, p145
SXSWi presentation by Brian Reynolds, Chief
Game Designer at Zygna,
11 March 2011
http://farmvillefreak.com, 11 March 2011
http://www.financemanila.net/2011/02/
how-does-zynga-make-money-their-business-
model-and-revenues/, 20 Feb 2011
http://www.examiner.com/farmville-in-
national/zynga-gamers-raise-1m-for-japan-
relief, 14 March 2011
http://www.associatedcontent.com/
article/7858698/social_gamers_of_zyngas_
farmville_can.html, 15 March 2011

Watermark Rum, p149
Cannes 2011 entry form
http://www.fasterlouder.com.au/news/
local/28021/Watermark-gigs-raise-money-
for-flood-relief, 4 April 2011

Plan-T, p150
Contagious Roundup 2010
Cannes 2011 entry form and case study video

Lufthansa Open Letter, p151
Email Nicola C. Lange
http://www.businessinsider.com/lufthansa-
offers-apples-iphone-losing-dude-a-free-
flight-to-germany-2010-4, 22 April

4th Amendment Wear, p154
Interview with Matt Ryan, Cannes,
23 July 2011
Phone interview with Tim Geoghegan,
September 2011
Cannes 2011 entry form and case study video

La Redoute, p158
http://www.stylist.co.uk/home/french-
fashion-chain-in-naked-blunder#image-
rotator-1
http://adage.com/article/global-news/
france-s-la-redoute-naked-guy-kids-fashion-
shoot/231927/

Mini Cooper Front, p159
http://www.independent.co.uk/news/world/
europe/its-a-mini-disaster-bmw-sponsors-
deadly-cold-front-6298210.html
http://www.bbc.co.uk/news/world-
europe-16852429
http://www.met.fu-berlin.de/adopt-a-vortex/
historie/
http://www.spiegel.de/international/europe/
marketing-mishap-european-cold-front-
cooper-sponsored-by-mini-a-812461.html

KFC Thailand, p159
http://thenextweb.com/facebook/
2012/04/12/facebook-faux-pas-thai-netizens-
cry-fowl-as-kfc-tells-public-to-order-chicken-
during-tsunami-scare/
http://www.huffingtonpost.co.uk/
2012/04/12/kfc-thailand-tells-customers-
pick-up-bucket-as-they-head-home-amid-
tsunami-threat_n_1420329.html
http://www.telegraph.co.uk/news/
worldnews/asia/thailand/9200106/KFC-
apologises-for-Thailand-earthquake-and-
tsunami-promotion.html

CHAPTER 7

Made in the Now quote, p160
Interview with Georgia Dixon

Michael Hyatt quote, p162
Platform: Get Noticed in a Noisy World,
Thomas Nelson, 2012

The Artistifier, p163
Interview with Jon Plackett, 22 July 2012
http://theartistifier.com/
http://www.neatorama.com/2012/02/28/
the-artistifier/

The Feed, p164
http://thefeed.orange.co.uk/
Interview with Ed Barrett, animator on
The Feed

Dan Schawbel quote, p164
www.personalbrandingblog.com/quotes/

Made in the Now, p165
Interview with Georgia Dixon, 19 June 2011
http://theweekendedition.com.au/
gentleman/made-in-the-now-turns-current-
events-into-fashion/

Call the Shots, p166
Interview with Kevin McGlade, 20 July 2012
iris-worldwide.com

Michael Hyatt quote, p167
http://www.aliventures.com/blogworld-
platform-michael-hyatt/

30 Days of Creativity, p169
http://30daysofcreativity.com/
http://blog.makezine.com/2010/06/01/30-
days-of-creativity-start-today/

F-ckYeah headlines, p175
http://f-ckyeahheadlines.com/
Skype interview with Eric Wedum,
5 April 2011

Recordsetter, p176
http://thenextweb.com/
shareables/2012/04/25/celebrate-
recordsetters-first-ever-world-record-day/
http://en.wikipedia.org/wiki/RecordSetter

CHAPTER 8

Marc Andreessen quote, p186
http://www.brainyquote.com/quotes/
authors/m/marc_andreessen_3.html

Grant McCracken quote, p189
http://timkastelle.org/blog/2012/05/
culturematic-by-grant-mccracken-makes-a-
great-case-for-experimenting/

Bumblecart, p190
Interview with Andy Pilkington

ACKNOWLEDGMENTS

PICTURE CREDITS

GRANT would like to say special thanks to his two girls, Caroline and Jia – sorry for the late nights and lost weekends. Co-author Jonathan David Burkhart for introducing me to SXSWi, coining Urgent Genius and applying it to what's new and next. And for being enthusiastic and a bit crazy. And for driving me crazy. Andy Nethercleft for helping sort out the layout and making sense of our chaotic writing; Jaina and Alex for putting me in contact with Mark at Crease Lightning who created the awesome origami gun; Joe Kerrigan for retouching the Urgent Genius newspaper on to the above-mentioned gun; The Urgent Genius panelists at SXSWi 2012: Michael Logan, Remco Marinus, @BronxZoosCobra and Esty Gorman.

JON will die a slow painful death inside if he doesn't send a special thanks to: Jo, my long-suffering wife and my two melanin-rich kids Olivia and Toby for putting up with months if not years of madness; my co-author Grant for his patience and tireless efforts initiating this tome and spearheading the launch and upkeep of the blog. For editing help in the last few months, I would have been stuck without the mad skills and home-brewing talents of newest Urgent Genius crew member Guy Galloway. I also depended on and am very grateful for the editing talents of my wife Jo, Andrew Green and Katie Garner. And I can't forget those I've placed on Team Sanity – those who contributed to keeping me almost sane. Matt Bateman and his wife Sarah gave up their home on a few occasions to provide me with a bit of kid-free space to think and find new ways to be distracted. Steve Rutterford, Louisa St Pierre and Steve Cole had several long chats with me from both New York and London and served as voices of reason in the midst of the panic. For the initial encouragement to get into advertising and learn the rules so you could break them, thanks to Jelly Helm and the folks at VCU Brandcenter. For keeping me in London and in advertising (and/or skirting around its edges), thanks to Chas 'Chesterfield' Bayfield. For several meet-ups when she lived in London and for helping me keep focused on finding 'my thing' and pursue it intently, thanks Jessica Hagy. For encouraging me to find suitors for my love of 'what's new and next' I must thank my SXSW 2013 co-speaker Steve Henry and the guys at Decoded.

BOTH GRANT AND JON would like to thank Ian Millner, Sean Reynolds and everyone at iris worldwide who has helped make Urgent Genius happen; our publisher Andrew Sanigar and editor Ruth Patrick at Thames & Hudson for their belief and patience; Jonny Plackett for inspiring us to create Urgent Genius; Roisin Kiberd for her super-quick editing, research and writing skills over the first year of the project. John Murphy for stepping in and designing a page or two when the deadline loomed. For all those who helped launch Urgent Genius on both Weekenders: Rob Luciani, Martin Butcher, Kara Lee Burke, Matt Diffee, Mark Sephton, Kevin McGlade, Joe Jacobs, Tom Prendergast, Nick Mack, Jay Fretwell, Paul Curry, Danny Fagerson, Jon Rosen, Mary Crosse, Will Saunders, Jon Aird, Will Cooke, Liz Pavitt, Matt Golding, Chris Quigley, Tif Slama, Aaron Sanchez, Carly Williams, Tian Murphy, Ant Melder, Tim Holden, Bill Adcock, Ashley Taylor, Tom Ormes, Subha Naidu, Jimmy Lee, Jonathan Cockett, Chris Shie, Shehan Karunatilaka, Paul Gage, Lucas Burrows, the iris Singapore gang, Miami Ad School/The Bunker, BBC Comedy, Rubber Republic's Kitten Camp, South By Southwest Interactive organizers and London College of Communication's Interaction and Moving Image department including tutors Alex Williamson and Joel Karamath. And finally, for helping to elevate newsjacking as a legitimate practice and for inspiring us with his Real-time Power Law way back in 2010, hats off to author and speaker David Meerman Scott.

INDEX